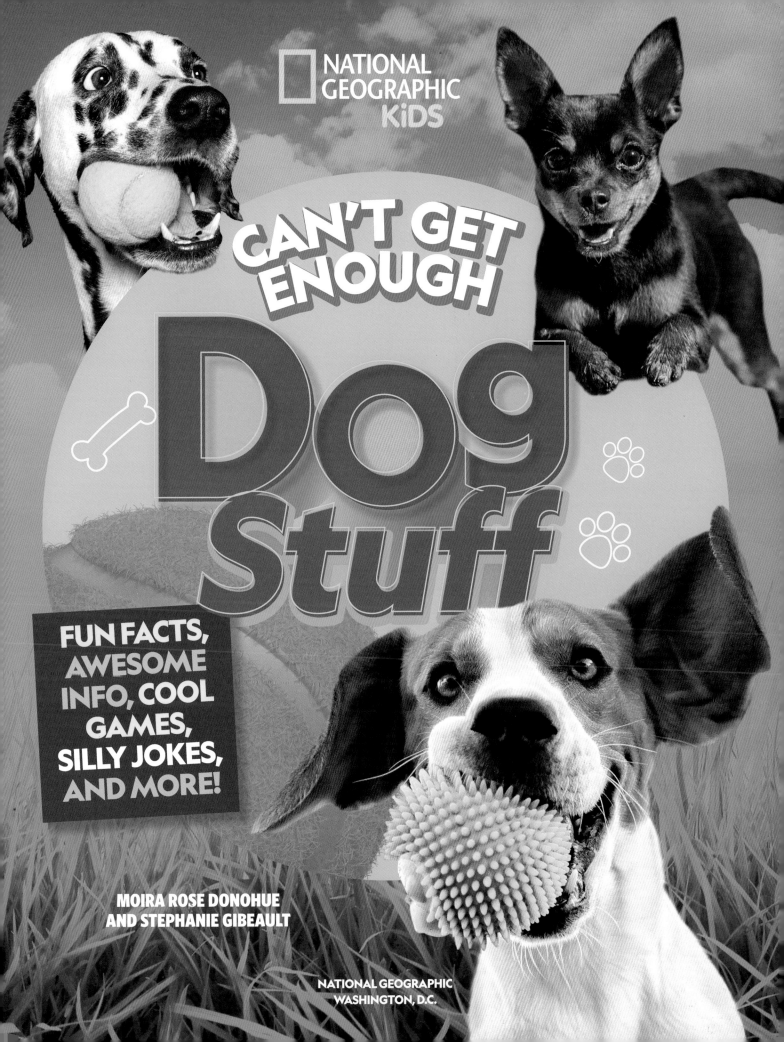

NATIONAL
GEOGRAPHIC
KiDS

CAN'T GET ENOUGH

Dog Stuff

FUN FACTS, AWESOME INFO, COOL GAMES, SILLY JOKES, AND MORE!

MOIRA ROSE DONOHUE
AND STEPHANIE GIBEAULT

NATIONAL GEOGRAPHIC
WASHINGTON, D.C.

TABLE OF CONTENTS

PREPARE FOR POOCHES!

WOOF! Dogs are popular pets all over the world. They cuddle on couches, hike over hills, chase down Frisbees, and sometimes even sleep on our beds. And they come in all shapes and sizes, ranging from tiny toy breeds to mammoth mutts. Dogs have been our constant companions for thousands of years, and there's almost no end to the jobs they do for us. It's no wonder we call them our best friends!

This book is your ulti-mutt source for dog fun. Inside, you'll fetch plenty of dog facts, such as which breeds are the fastest and how dogs hear. Dig into quizzes to test your canine cleverness and chase laughs with plenty of jokes. Sniff out stories about how dogs think and experience the world, read interviews with canine experts, and discover dog world-record holders. Plus, enjoy canine crafts and puppy puzzles, such as word scrambles and matching games. Not sure how to pronounce a breed name? Check out the pronunciation guide on pages 122–123. No bones about it—you'll have a howling good time!

SPEAK DOG!

ou can learn to speak "dog" in no time. On a separate piece of paper, write the numbers from 1–20. Fetch the definitions from the boxes on the right and match them with the dog-related words on the left. Write the letter next to the appropriate number. Then compare them to the answer key on page 9.

1 BREED	**2** CANIDAE	**3** COGNITION	**4** CONES
5 DEWCLAW	**6** DOMESTICATION	**7** FLEWS	**8** HOCK
9 INSTINCT	**10** JACOBSON'S ORGAN	**11** LITTER	**12** PREY
13 PRICK EARS	**14** SCAVENGER	**15** SERVICE DOG	**16** STIFLE
17 SUBMISSIVE	**18** TICKING	**19** TOY DOG	**20** VETERINARIAN

A
A natural behavior

B
A dog's knee

C
An animal hunted by another for food

D
The thick, hanging upper lips of a dog

E
Puppies born at the same time to the same mother

F
The scientific family of animals that includes dogs, wolves, and jackals

G
A doctor who treats animals

H
An animal that feeds on dead animals

I
Ears that are pointed or standing up stiffly

J
An extra claw on the inside of a dog's leg; a "fifth toe"

K
Small flecks of a different color on a dog's coat, like freckles

L
A dog trained to help an owner with a disability

M
A small pet dog

N
Cells in the eye that let most animals see color

O
Recognizing that someone else is in charge

P
The process of learning or thinking

Q
The bones that form a dog's ankle

R
The process in which animals are tamed to live with humans

S
A group or type of dog with a similar appearance

T
A nasal sac that helps animals, especially dogs, smell

HOUND HUMOR

KNOCK, KNOCK.

Who's there?
Howl.
Howl who?
Howl will you know
if you don't open
the door?

Q

Why did the
skeleton fall
down?

A

His dog kept
stealing his
bones.

CONNOR: Why did the golden retriever fail to catch
the squirrel?

RODRIGO: I don't know. Why?

CONNOR: It was barking up the wrong tree!

Q Why is a Dalmatian so bad at hide-and-seek?

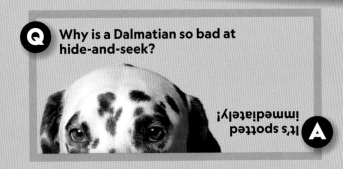

A It's spotted immediately!

Q What's a dog's favorite holiday?

A Howl-o-ween.

Q What says nothing but gives dogs all the local gossip?

A Peemail.

DOG 1: What's the worst part about being a famous dog?

DOG 2: The puparazzi!

11

FIDO'S FORM

Dogs come in so many shapes and sizes! Yet they all have the same basic physical structure. Many of their body parts are like those people have, but the names we use for them are different. Look at this drawing of a dog's body to learn the lingo.

Muzzle (nose and mouth)
Also known as the snout, the muzzle is where you'll find a dog's greatest tool: its nose! Like humans, dogs have special tiny body parts, called olfactory cells, inside their noses. These cells detect scents, but dogs have millions more of these odor-detecting cells in their noses than humans do. Because their nostrils work independently, dogs can tell if a smell is coming from their right or their left.

Flews (upper lips)
Some breeds like the Dogue de Bordeaux have flews that are so droopy they form jowls. The flews provide protection for the mouth and may help funnel scents to the nose. But watch out—this is the body part responsible for flinging drool!

Dewclaw (thumb)
A dewclaw is an extra claw on the inside of the front leg. Some breeds have them on their rear legs, too. They are the doggy version of thumbs or big toes. Although dogs can't text with them, dewclaws may provide traction when running and might help dogs hold objects like bones.

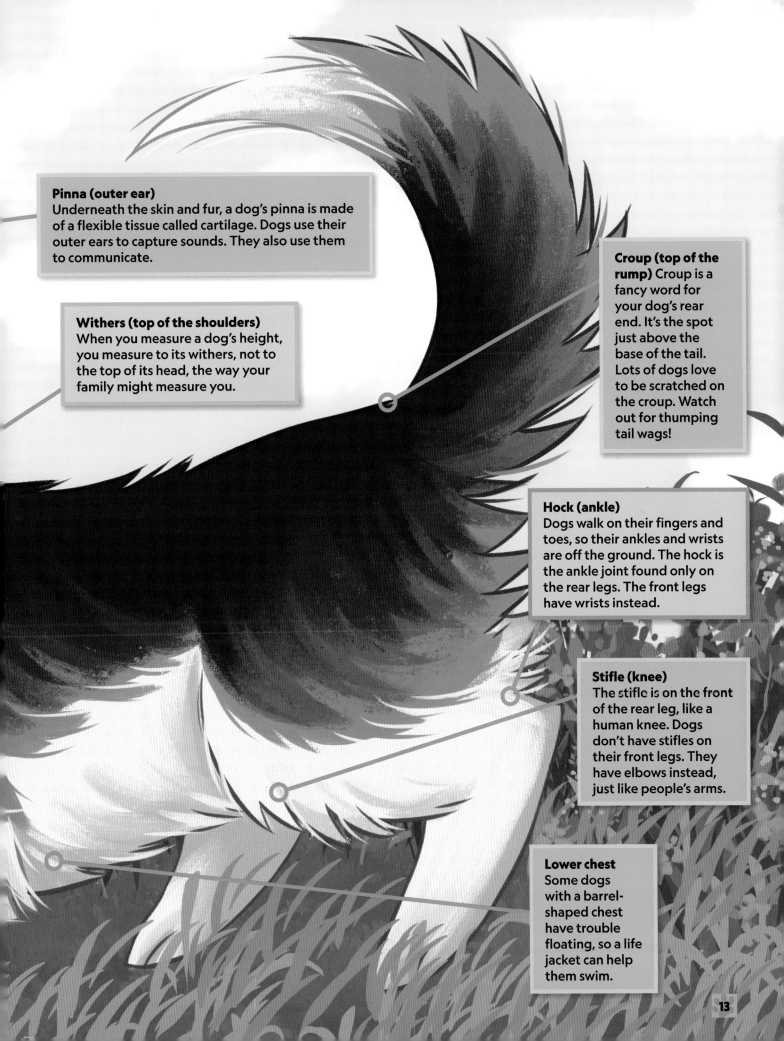

Pinna (outer ear)
Underneath the skin and fur, a dog's pinna is made of a flexible tissue called cartilage. Dogs use their outer ears to capture sounds. They also use them to communicate.

Withers (top of the shoulders)
When you measure a dog's height, you measure to its withers, not to the top of its head, the way your family might measure you.

Croup (top of the rump) Croup is a fancy word for your dog's rear end. It's the spot just above the base of the tail. Lots of dogs love to be scratched on the croup. Watch out for thumping tail wags!

Hock (ankle)
Dogs walk on their fingers and toes, so their ankles and wrists are off the ground. The hock is the ankle joint found only on the rear legs. The front legs have wrists instead.

Stifle (knee)
The stifle is on the front of the rear leg, like a human knee. Dogs don't have stifles on their front legs. They have elbows instead, just like people's arms.

Lower chest
Some dogs with a barrel-shaped chest have trouble floating, so a life jacket can help them swim.

13

WHAT'S IN A BREED?

MOST DOG BREEDS HAVE BEEN AROUND FOR LESS THAN 200 YEARS.

TODAY THERE ARE OVER 470 MILLION PET DOGS WORLDWIDE.

CANINES HAVE LIVED ON THE PLANET FOR A LONG TIME.

Dogs, the domesticated descendants of wolves, have been hanging out with humans for at least 14,000 years! Scientists think the ancient Egyptians may have been the first people to breed dogs for specific purposes. To create strong guard dogs, they bred loud, stocky dogs together. This led to breeds like the mastiff. They also picked slender, agile dogs and bred them together. These dogs made good hunters. The saluki probably came from these ancient Egyptian dogs.

NEW BREEDS

Through the years, people continued to breed dogs for their traits and their ability to do jobs such as tracking and herding. But by the 1800s, people had begun breeding "man's best friend" not just for what dogs could do, but also for how they looked. They picked features, such as long snouts or short tails, because they liked the appearance. Then they bred dogs with those traits together. These breeders and owners formed "kennel clubs." Kennel clubs are still around today. They set breed standards for how they think breeds should look and behave. They keep track of each dog's family tree, which is called a pedigree. Most U.S. kennel clubs divide dogs into seven groups related to their abilities: sporting, herding, hounds (trackers), terriers (hunters), working, non-sporting, and toy. The non-sporting group includes dogs with abilities that don't fit into the other categories, such as watchdogs. What's the job of a dog in the toy group? Toy dogs are small dogs bred to cuddle!

BEST BREEDS

Today there are around 400 breeds recognized worldwide. But pedigreed dogs are not the only kinds of pet dogs. Purebred dogs don't have pedigree papers, but they have parents of the same breed. Mixed breeds, or mutts, have parents from different breeds or parents that are mixed breeds, too. Designer dogs are the result of dogs from different breeds being crossed on purpose to create something new, like a labradoodle or a cockapoo. What's the best breed? That's easy—whatever dog is sticking its wet nose in your hand!

BOTH GREAT DANES AND ROTTWEILERS ARE THOUGHT TO BE DESCENDANTS OF AN ANCIENT DOG BREED, THE MOLOSSUS, THAT NO LONGER EXISTS.

BEST IN SHOW

SOME DOG BREEDS ARE FAMOUS FOR JUMPING HIGH OR RUNNING FAST. BUT SOME BREEDS HAVE MORE UNUSUAL TALENTS!

🏅 BEST SLEEPER

BASSET HOUND

Adult dogs generally sleep between 12 and 14 hours a day. But basset hounds like their z's. These low-slung couch potatoes can snooze 13 to 18 hours a day. Watch out, though—when they are following a scent, these hounds can go the distance!

🏅 BEST DIGGER

BEAGLE

Beagles hunt for underground prey, so they are exceptional diggers. They like to dig holes to bury bones, too. Burying bones is an instinct passed down from wolves, which bury food to make sure they will have something to eat if prey is scarce.

🏅 BEST ESCAPE ARTIST

BOXER

Some dogs dig their way out of the yard. But the boxer bounces! Boxers can leap over a four-foot (1.2 m)-tall fence in a single bound and can sometimes climb fences as high as six feet (1.8 m). Boxers got their name because they protect themselves with their front feet, like human boxers do.

BEST DROOLER

NEAPOLITAN MASTIFF

Neapolitan mastiffs have thick hanging lips, called flews. Sometimes when they shake their heads, gobs of slobber fly. The Neapolitan is an ancient dog bred to help guard the Roman Empire. It can weigh up to 150 pounds (68 kg). But don't be fooled by its size—it's a gentle giant.

BEST-NAMED CANINE

IT'S A TIE!

The Dandie Dinmont terrier was named after a fictional character in a novel from 1815. Say its name aloud and you'll surely giggle. The Petit Basset Griffon Vendéen's name translates to small (petit) low (basset) shaggy (griffon) dog from the Vendée region of France. It's usually called the PBGV or "the happy breed."

PETIT BASSET
GRIFFON VENDÉEN

DANDIE DINMONT

HOME SWEET HOME

Dogs live all over the world! Wherever you find people, you will find dogs. And there are hundreds of different breeds. Although you can find most breeds just about anywhere, each one was first developed in a particular part of the globe. This map shows the original home of seven breeds.

Breed: Alaskan malamute

Where: Northwestern Alaska, U.S.A.

Original Purpose: Pulling sledges and carrying packs

Fun Facts: These dogs are named for the Mahlemiut, an Inuit people who also used them to search for seals under the ice.

Northwestern Alaska, U.S.A.

NORTH AMERICA

PACIFIC OCEAN

ATLANTIC OCEAN

PERU

SOUTH AMERICA

SOUTHERN OCEAN

Breed: Peruvian Inca Orchid

Where: Peru

Original Purpose: Pets for various Indigenous peoples in what is now Peru

Fun Facts: Usually hairless, they were once thought to bring good health. Pottery from more than a thousand years ago features images of these dogs in sweaters!

Breed: Azawakh

Where: South Sahara, Africa

Original Purpose: Guarding tents, herding flocks, and hunting

Fun Facts: These dogs were traditionally owned by the nomadic, or traveling, Tuareg people. They have long legs and are extremely lean because they need speed and endurance in the hot, dry desert.

Breed: Great Dane
Where: Germany
Original Purpose: Hunting boar
Fun Facts: Great Danes aren't Danish at all! In 1876, they were named the national dog of Germany. Germans call them Deutsche Dogge, which means German mastiff.

Breed: Akita
Where: Northern Japan
Original Purpose: Hunting wild game such as boar, deer, and even bears
Fun Facts: At one time, only samurai and Japanese nobility were allowed to own an Akita. Later, the emperor changed the law so everybody could have them as pets.

Breed: Australian cattle dog
Where: Western interior of Australia
Original Purpose: Herding cattle
Fun Facts: These dogs are also known as blue heelers. They were developed for harsh terrain and high temperatures by breeding collies with a type of wild Australian dog called a dingo.

Breed: Coton de Tulear
Where: Madagascar
Original Purpose: Lapdogs for noble families
Fun Facts: These dogs are named "coton," French for cotton, after their soft, white coats. Legend has it that their ancestors swam to shore from a shipwreck and survived the wilderness by forming packs!

ARCTIC OCEAN

ASIA

GERMANY
EUROPE

Northern
JAPAN

South Sahara

PACIFIC
OCEAN

AFRICA

INDIAN
OCEAN

MADAGASCAR

Western
Interior,
AUSTRALIA

BREED BONANZA

Spanish and French explorers in what is now the United States crossbred their dogs from Europe with a native dog found in Louisiana. This created the first dog known to be bred in the U.S.: the CATAHOULA LEOPARD DOG. This canine was just right for SWAMP LIVING.

People bred NEWFOUNDLANDS to have partially webbed feet, which makes them perfect for RESCUING SWIMMERS.

The
LHASA APSO

may look like a cuddly teddy bear, but it was bred to guard Buddhist monks in eastern Asia. Its name can be translated as "bark lion guard dog."

Sight hounds—dogs that rely more on their vision than on their sense of smell to track animals, such as Afghan hounds— were bred for their super sight and can see 270 degrees around themselves without turning their heads.

SIBERIAN HUSKIES WERE BRED BY THE CHUKCHI PEOPLE FOR THEIR STRENGTH AND ENERGY. IN 1925, RELAY TEAMS OF THESE DOGS PULLED A SLED WITH LIFESAVING MEDICINE FOR A DISTANCE OF 674 MILES (1,085 KM).

Bred by **Lord Tweedmouth** of Great Britain, the golden retriever is a "soft-mouth" dog. It carries things gently in its mouth. No torn newspapers with this dog!

Sometimes called **WIENER DOGS,** low-to-the-ground dachshunds were originally bred to sniff out badgers.

The Lagotto Romagnolo was bred for its keen sense of smell. It can sniff out truffles, a rare mushroom used in fancy restaurants.

WHICH DOG BREED MATCHES YOUR PERSONALITY?

Dog breeds often have different personalities. Which one is most like you? To find out, answer these questions. Pick the best answer, but choose only one for each question. Write down the letter of each answer on a piece of paper. Your choices will reveal your dog identity. And remember, there are no right or wrong answers.

1. When your family watches a movie, you _____.

   a. call everyone together

   b. snuggle together under a blanket

   c. take breaks to stretch, fetch popcorn, and go to the bathroom

   d. make running jokes and howl with laughter

   e. do different things depending on the movie

2. In school, you _____.

   a. are usually the first person to raise your hand

   b. are happiest when sitting by your best friend

   c. like PE or sports the best

   d. are known as the class clown

   e. like to try out as many different things as you can

3. What is your favorite way to travel from one place to another?

   a. It doesn't matter how we travel, as long as everyone stays in line.

   b. walking

   c. a fast car or a jet plane

   d. a unicycle

   e. I'm happy going along with the pack.

4. How would you describe your eating habits?

   a. I'm a picky eater.

   b. I eat as much as I can get.

   c. I like anything that gives me energy.

   d. Snacks—the messier the better!

   e. I'll try anything once.

5. Which activity do you most prefer?

   a. playing quiz games

   b. hanging with my bestie

   c. skateboarding, swimming, and playing sports

   d. thinking up new jokes and pranks

   e. From playing to napping to snacking, I do it all!

6. What vacations do you like best?

a. camp, with planned activities

b. anywhere with my family

c. trips with adventurous activities, like zip-lining

d. trips to one-of-a-kind places

e. traveling somewhere new each time

7. Which career would you most like?

a. the leader of a country

b. a nurse

c. an Olympic athlete

d. a comedian

e. an archaeologist

8. If you were dressing up, which costume would you be most likely to pick?

a. superhero

b. giant panda

c. sports star

d. clown

e. part of a group costume with friends

CHECK YOUR SCORE. Count up how many of each letter you have chosen. Then read the results below. If you have a tie score, read the results for both letters:

Three or more a's:
You are most like a border collie.
Like you, the border collie is highly intelligent—as in rocket-scientist smart—and very observant. The border collie was bred in Great Britain to herd sheep. Unlike some other herding dogs, it keeps sheep together by staring at them. Do you have a laser stare, too?

Three or more b's:
You are most like an American Staffordshire terrier.
This dog is strong and muscular. But, just like you, it's a cuddle bug at heart! Also like you, it is a devoted pal that wants more than anything to spend time with its best friend.

Three or more c's:
You are most like a Jack Russell terrier.
Like you, the Jack Russell is full of energy and loves getting active. This dog was bred to chase and hunt burrowing prey, such as rats or foxes. It is smart and brave. You probably are, too!

Three or more d's:
You are most like a pug.
This ancient breed has been around for some 2,000 years! It was developed in China to be a companion. What does this little dog have in common with you? Well, you're social, playful, and friendly. And, like you, so is the pug, which is also sometimes silly and likes to clown around!

Three or more e's:
(or not three or more of anything):
You are most like a golden retriever.
You are cheerful and easy to get along with. So is the golden retriever! Lovable and loyal, it is one of the most popular breeds in the United States.

MUTT MAYHEM

Scientists can use a **dog's DNA** to find out what breeds are in its family history.

Mutts, also known as mixed breed dogs, can have **three or more breeds in their DNA.**

NATIONAL MUTT DAY IS CELEBRATED **TWICE A YEAR: ON JULY 31 AND DECEMBER 2.**

Just over half of all the dogs that live in people's homes are mutts. **At least 75 PERCENT OF THE DOGS IN SHELTERS ARE MIXED BREEDS** waiting to find their *furever* **home.**

The **"adoptable dog"** is the official state dog of Georgia, U.S.A.

MIXED BREED PUPPIES

can be a fun mystery. Without knowing their breed makeup, it's hard to predict how big they will grow, what they will look like, and how they will act as adults.

Until 2014, mutts weren't allowed to compete in many official dog sport competitions, but now they can go head-to-head with purebreds!

Do you want a dog that is different from every other dog in the park? **CHOOSE A MUTT!** You will get a blend of breeds for a one-of-a-kind look and personality.

DO YOU SMELL THAT?

Have you ever watched a puppy look in the mirror? It's hilarious! They bark and bounce trying to get the "other" dog to play. How can they get so confused? Well, recognizing yourself in the mirror is a special ability that few types of animals seem to have. It's called self-recognition. Scientists usually test for this ability with something called the mirror test. First, they make a mark on the animal's body with a safe dye. Then they have the animal look in a mirror. If the animal inspects the mark on its own, real body after seeing it in the mirror, this means it recognizes itself in the mirror reflection.

ASKING THE RIGHT QUESTION

Does this mean that dogs can't recognize themselves at all? Not necessarily. Dogs rely on their noses more than their eyes. Asking them to examine themselves in a mirror is like asking you to pick an outfit by smelling your clothes. It makes no sense! So scientists developed a different test to see if dogs have self-recognition. This is called the sniff test. The scientists showed dogs several containers that held cotton pads soaked in pee. One container held the sniffer's own pee, and the rest held pee from other dogs. Then the scientists measured how long the dogs spent smelling each container.

PEE-YEW!

The result? The dogs spent more time smelling the other dogs' pee than their own. This shows they aren't as interested in their own scent because they know it so well. In other words, they recognize it. Then, to mimic the mirror test, scientists took it up a notch. They showed the dogs two containers, both of which held the dog's own pee. But an extra smell was added to the pee in one of the two containers. This change was just like the mark on the body in the mirror test. And guess what? Dogs spent more time smelling the changed pee than the unchanged pee. They knew something was different about their own smell.

It seems dogs do have self-recognition. At least, as long as their noses are involved. And that might mean dogs have self-awareness. That's the ability to think about yourself and your own feelings and behavior as different from the thoughts, feelings, and behavior of others. And that's a special skill indeed.

JUST LIKE PUPPIES, HUMAN BABIES CAN'T RECOGNIZE THEMSELVES IN A MIRROR!

EVERY YEAR, OVER

3 MILLION DOGS ARE ADOPTED

FROM RESCUE ORGANIZATIONS AND SHELTERS.

LOTS OF RESCUE GROUPS MAKE SOCIAL MEDIA PROFILES FOR THEIR DOGS THAT NEED HOMES—WHICH CAN INCREASE ADOPTIONS BY MORE THAN 66 PERCENT!

TIPPING THE SCALES

Some dogs are teeny-tiny, and other dogs are giants. Some pups are short and sturdy while others are tall and lean. Want to see how heavy different breeds are? Take a look at the weight of some dogs compared with objects that are as heavy as they are. Then you can really see who is tipping the scales!

Great Dane
WEIGHT: **up to 175 pounds (79 kg)**
THAT'S ABOUT AS HEAVY AS: **6 standard solid gold bars**

Basset hound
WEIGHT: **up to 65 pounds (29 kg)**
THAT'S ABOUT AS HEAVY AS: **1 gas-powered push lawn mower**

Mastiff

WEIGHT: up to 230 pounds (104 kg)

THAT'S ABOUT AS HEAVY AS: 1 giant panda

West Highland white terrier

WEIGHT: up to 20 pounds (9 kg)

THAT'S ABOUT AS HEAVY AS: 20 cans of soup

Chihuahua

WEIGHT: up to 6 pounds (2.7 kg)

THAT'S ABOUT AS HEAVY AS: 3 guinea pigs

Bernese mountain dog

WEIGHT: up to 115 pounds (52 kg)

THAT'S ABOUT AS HEAVY AS: 4 car tires

DOG-EARED

Dogs have more than 12 muscles in their outer ears. Humans have only three.

When a **dog tilts its head,** it may be trying to figure out where a **sound is coming from.**

DOGS **"SPEAK"** THROUGH THEIR EARS. FLATTENED EARS USUALLY MEAN THE DOG IS AFRAID, WHILE EARS **UP AND FORWARD** SHOW THAT THE DOG IS **PAYING ATTENTION.**

IF YOUR **DOG RUNS AWAY** FROM THE VACUUM CLEANER, IT'S PROBABLY BECAUSE IT SOUNDS **MUCH NOISIER** TO HER THAN TO YOU.

Dogs can hear sounds pitched more than twice as high as what most adult humans can hear.

PUPPIES are **BORN DEAF** but usually can hear within a few weeks.

Think there might be termites nearby? Ask your dog! Many dogs can actually hear them chomping on **wood.**

DOGS CAN MOVE THEIR EARS SEPARATELY and can turn **ONE EAR** toward a specific sound.

(Human can't do that with their ears!)

The record for the **LONGEST DOG EAR IS 13.5 INCHES (34.3 CM). That's more than a foot long!**

Turn the page for more ear-raising facts about dog ears!

Prick ears, which stand straight up, were inherited from wolf ancestors.

LONG, "DROP" EARS, SOMETIMES CALLED PENDANT EARS, AREN'T JUST FOR HEARING. THEY STIR UP SMELLS ON THE GROUND TO HELP SOME HOUNDS SNIFF OUT SMELLS.

Dogs **CAN HEAR NOISES** made by the tiny machine parts inside computers and phones.

THE PAPILLON HAS EARS THAT LOOK LIKE THEY COULD BE USED AS **WINGS TO FLY!** THESE ARE CALLED BUTTERFLY EARS.

Only the Bedlington terrier has filbert-shaped ears, named after the shape of the nuts that grow on the filbert, or hazelnut, tree.

Some dogs have **blunt ears** that stand up and have rounded tips. Really large blunt ears are sometimes called bat ears.

Button ears stand up at the base, but the flap folds over and covers the ear canal.

Some researchers think dogs may be able to **HEAR EARTHQUAKES** before we can!

Dog ears that fold backward are called rose ears.

SERVICE DOG SCIENCE

GITA GNANADESIKAN, DOG SCIENTIST

Gita adopted two kittens in high school, one outgoing and the other shy. Ever since, she has been curious about the personalities of animals. Now, she's exploring the behavior and training of service dogs. Service dogs do specific jobs to help people with disabilities, such as opening a door for someone who uses a wheelchair. To find out more about how dogs learn and what makes a great service dog, Gita studies both puppies and adult dogs.

WHY DO YOU STUDY SERVICE DOGS?

The waiting list for a service dog is often a couple of years long. And only about half of the dogs that are trained actually pass their tests. We hope our research will help service dog organizations breed and train more dogs to help people with all sorts of tasks, from picking up dropped objects to pulling someone in a wheelchair.

WHAT KINDS OF EXPERIMENTS DO YOU DO?

Many of our experiments involve hiding treats and seeing how the dogs solve the problem. Sometimes we just interact with the dogs and see how they react. In a particularly fun task that I designed, we talk to puppies in a high-pitched voice for 30 seconds and measure how much eye contact they make with us.

WHAT DO YOU HOPE TO DISCOVER?

We are hoping to learn what makes a good service dog. But we also want to understand dog behavior in general. Why is one dog really interested in playing fetch and learning names for its toys while another is less interested in people but great at solving puzzles? We're also interested in learning what makes a dog a dog, as opposed to a wolf. Dogs were domesticated from wolves at least 14,000 years ago. Their skeletons, fur color, digestion, and behavior have all changed greatly over that time. But we're still learning what those differences are and how they evolved.

WHAT'S THE BEST PART OF YOUR RESEARCH?

There are constant funny and sweet moments when you work with dogs. When we do our experiments with young puppies, we sit on the floor with them. They like to lick our faces, clamber into our laps, and sometimes even chew on our hands, toes, and noses. The hardest part is trying to not laugh in the middle of an experiment!

WHAT DO YOU LOVE ABOUT BEING A SCIENTIST?

One of the most exciting parts of being a scientist is learning something about how the world works that no one else knows yet. I didn't realize as a kid how much we still don't know.

DOGS ARE WONDERFUL RESEARCH SUBJECTS BECAUSE THEY ARE EAGER TO PARTICIPATE, ARE EXCITED BY PRAISE, AND LOVE TO SEARCH FOR HIDDEN TREATS.

IN THIS EXPERIMENT, SCIENTISTS HIDE A PIECE OF FOOD UNDER ONE OF THE TWO CUPS. THEN THEY POINT AT A CUP AND WATCH TO SEE IF THE PUPPY CHOOSES THE CUP THEY ARE POINTING AT OR CHOOSES AT RANDOM.

CANINE COMEDY

Q What's Lassie's favorite vegetable?

A Collieflower.

Q Why do Dalmatians like Morse code?

A All the dots and dashes!

Q What kind of day is it when a dog can't catch a rabbit?

A A bad hare day.

TONGUE TWISTER

SAY THIS FAST THREE TIMES:
The fox outfoxed five foxhounds.

LAUGHABLE LIST

A Dog's Favorite Foods:

Chow chow mein

....

Pugsghetti

....

Muttsarella cheese

....

Q What has all bark but no bite?

A A dogwood tree.

Q What dog makes the best pastry?

A A Great Danish.

OMAR: Guess what?

MARISOL: What?

OMAR: Puppy butt!

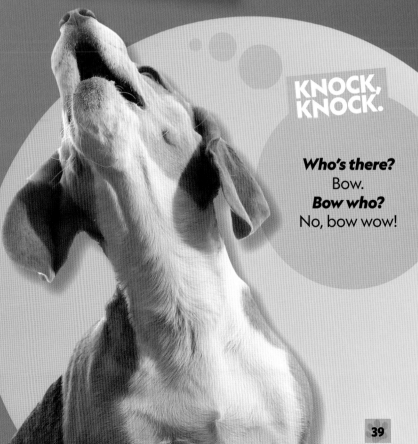

KNOCK, KNOCK.

Who's there?
Bow.
Bow who?
No, bow wow!

DIY SNUFFLE MAT

IF YOU DON'T HAVE A DOG TO PLAY WITH, CONSIDER DONATING YOUR SNUFFLE MAT TO A RESCUE ORGANIZATION OR ANIMAL SHELTER. THE DOGS THERE WILL LOVE HAVING FUN WITH YOUR TOY.

Dogs use their noses to interact with the world and find food. Toys and games that allow dogs to use their sense of smell are lots of fun and a good brain workout. In fact, challenging a dog's super sniffer prevents boredom and stress. To give a dog a chance to use its powerful nose, try making this snuffle mat toy.

STEP 1:

Either tear the fleece or T-shirt material into strips or have an adult help you cut it. Make each strip one inch (2.5 cm) wide and around seven inches (18 cm) long. You will need almost twice as many strips as there are holes in your mat.

YOU WILL NEED:

FLEECE MATERIAL
(AT LEAST A YARD/METER)
OR SEVERAL OLD T-SHIRTS
SCISSORS
PLASTIC MAT WITH HOLES IN
IT (SUCH AS A SINK MAT OR A
RUBBER ANTI-FATIGUE MAT)
DOG TREATS (OPTIONAL)

STEP 2:

Push one end of a strip through the first hole in the mat. Then push the other end of the strip through the hole under the first. Flip the mat over and tie a knot in the loose ends so the knot is tight against the mat and the ends hang. Now flip the mat over again. Take another strip and push one end through the second hole beside the first strip. Then push the other end through the third hole. Flip the mat over and tie a knot in the second strip. Repeat this process all the way across the mat for each row of holes. Make sure all the knots are on the same side of the mat.

STEP 3:

When you're finished, the back side of the mat should be a flat grid of crisscrossed strips. The front side should be a fluffy carpet of fleece.

CONCLUSION:

Now you're ready to play with a dog. For the first game, simply toss a few dog treats on top of the mat and let the dog eat them. This will teach the dog that the mat contains treats. After that, you can make the game harder by hiding treats inside the strips so the dog has to sniff them out. Watch how quickly they can find all the treats!

FOR SAFETY, ALWAYS WATCH A DOG WHEN THEY PLAY WITH A SNUFFLE MAT TO BE SURE THEY DON'T TRY TO EAT THE STRIPS.

DOG OR SHEEP?

THE KOMONDOR WAS BRED TO BLEND IN WITH FLOCKS OF SHEEP. ITS **UNIQUE LOOK LETS IT HIDE UNDERCOVER** TO WATCH FOR PREDATORS AND THEN **SCARE THEM AWAY.**

THIS **"MOP" DOG'S FUR** GROWS IN CLUMPS OR ROPE-LIKE CORDS. IT NEVER NEEDS BRUSHING, EVEN AFTER A BATH!

DOGS VS. CATS

SWORN ENEMIES?

Do dogs and cats really hate each other? The answer is NO! But while they may not be mortal enemies, they aren't always best friends, either. Why? To begin with, they are different species. Dogs are members of the family Canidae, which includes wolves. Cats, like lions, are from the Felidae family. Put a lion and a wolf together, and the lion would have dinner! But don't worry. Domesticated cats and dogs—those we keep as pets—don't have to eat each other. Both are fed by humans and don't need to hunt for meals!

WHILE MOST DOGS SLEEP AROUND 12 TO 14 HOURS A DAY, CATS CATNAP FOR AROUND 15 TO 18 HOURS.

CAT TONGUES ARE COVERED IN BACKWARD-FACING SPINES TO GROOM THEIR FUR; DOGS HAVE SMOOTH TONGUES.

CUT TO THE CHASE

If dogs and cats don't necessarily see each other as snacks, why do dogs chase cats? Dogs race after anything that moves—balls, squirrels, and yes, cats. It's an instinct—a behavior they are born with. Cats, on the other hand, wait and pounce on prey. That's an instinct, too. These two behaviors don't go together all that well.

On top of that, cats and dogs communicate differently. A wagging dog tail means the dog is happy. A twitchy cat tail signals that it's ready to attack. And cats tend to be loners while dogs are happiest as part of a pack.

GETTING ALONG

Can these two different species live together in the same house without "fighting like cats and dogs"? The best chance for success is to start when both animals are young. Getting a puppy and a kitten at the same time usually sets them up to live peacefully together. Introducing a kitten or puppy to a much older, calmer animal of the other species can work, too. Eventually, the two pets learn to respect each other. And sometimes ... they even become besties.

CANINE COMEDY

KNOCK, KNOCK.

Who's there?
Bichon.
Bichon who?
It's so hot, let's go to the bichon Friday.

Q What instrument did the dog learn to play?

A The trombone.

Q What do you call a dog doctor after a swim?

A A veterinarian.

TONGUE TWISTER

SAY THIS FAST THREE TIMES:

The singing springer spaniel sprang.

A Dog's Favorite Artists:

Leonardo Dog Vinci
....

Henri Muttisse
....

Andy Warhowl
....

JAYDEN: Wow—it's raining cats and dogs!

RAVI: How do you know?

JAYDEN: I just stepped on a poodle.

RIDDLE ME THIS...

Q What's red, has 400 paws, and barks?

A 100 Irish setters begging for a treat.

Q What do you call a dog that likes spicy food?

A A chili dog.

47

WAGGIEST TAILS

🎗 FUNNIEST TAIL

AUSTRALIAN STUMPY TAIL CATTLE DOG

Paws down, the funniest tail belongs to the Australian stumpy tail cattle dog. Cattle dogs come in two varieties— long-tailed and stumpy-tailed. But when breeders stopped breeding the dogs with the nubby tails, they almost disappeared. Luckily, in the 1980s, the Australian National Kennel Council began work to preserve this dog variety.

🎗 PUFFIEST TAIL

CHOW CHOW

Look closely—buried in all the chow chow's fluffy fur is a poofy, puffy tail. Some think the chow chow looks like a lion. But others think it looks more like a giant panda, which, like the chow chow, comes from China.

LONGEST TAIL

IRISH WOLFHOUND

The tallest breed of dogs, Irish wolfhounds have long, slightly curved tails. One Irish wolfhound has a tail that stretches to 30.2 inches (76. 8 cm). That's about as long as the dog is tall, from shoulder to toe. And probably long enough to clear a coffee table in one wag!

WAGGIEST TAIL

GOLDEN RETRIEVER

Which dog has the waggiest tail? If you've ever met a golden retriever, you know the answer. Goldens wave their feathery plumed tails a lot. They use them to show that they are happy, for balance, and as a rudder to help steer when they are dog-paddling.

CURLIEST TAIL

SHIBA INU

The Shiba Inu comes from the mountains of Japan. Dogs from cold regions often have curly tails. Why? So they can keep their noses warm when they curl up for a nap. Check out this dog's tail— it has an impressive twirl.

MIXED-UP PUPS

These pups have gotten a little confused. Read the hints, then unscramble the letters to help them find their true identities. Write your answers on a separate piece of paper and compare them to the answer key at the bottom of the page.

1 ANNIMOPERA
(HINT: SHAKE YOUR POMPOMS!)

ADULT DOGS HAVE 42 TEETH. HUMAN ADULTS ONLY HAVE 32.

2 FISTMAF
(HINT: IT'S MASSIVE!)

3 ZACHUNERS
(HINT: RHYMES WITH YOWZER.)

50

HUMANS HAVE SOME 9,000 TASTE BUDS. DOGS ONLY HAVE ABOUT 1,700. BUT UNLIKE HUMANS, THEY HAVE SPECIAL TASTE BUDS THAT LET THEM TASTE WATER!

4 ROXBE
(HINT: IT PACKS A PUNCH.)

5 SHINGLE RESTTE
(HINT: IT'S SET FOR TEA.)

6 RETNIOP
(HINT: IT CAN SHOW YOU THE WAY.)

7 ERCCOK ELIPANS
(HINT: THE FIRST PART SOUNDS LIKE A ROCKER.)

8 ONLAPLIP
(HINT: IT HAS BUTTERFLY EARS.)

A NOSE FOR SNOW

To teach **avalanche dogs to dig in the snow,** trainers bury a rag. When the dogs dig it up, they get to **play tug-of-war!**

Saint Bernard dogs can help save people trapped by avalanches. They can smell a person buried under as much as 20 feet (6.1 m) of snow.

AVALANCHE DOGS CAN **SEARCH 2.5 ACRES (1 HA) IN ABOUT 30 MINUTES.** IT WOULD TAKE 20 PEOPLE EIGHT TIMES AS LONG TO COVER THE SAME AREA!

Avalanche dogs start their day with a **full, fatty breakfast**—such as bacon!—to prepare them for a long day of work.

AVALANCHE RESCUE DOGS OFTEN START TRAINING AS PUPPIES. IT CAN TAKE A YEAR, OR EVEN LONGER, TO GRADUATE DOG **RESCUE TRAINING.**

DOG BREEDS THAT ARE GOOD AT LOCATING PEOPLE TRAPPED IN SNOW ARE GOLDEN RETRIEVERS, GERMAN SHEPHERDS, COLLIES, LABRADOR RETRIEVERS, AND, OF COURSE, SAINT BERNARDS.

By tunneling through 200 feet (60 m) of snow, a wolf-dog hybrid named Shana led her owners, Eve and Norman Fertig, to safety when they were trapped by a snowstorm.

Avalanche dogs are comfortable RIDING ON SNOWMOBILES, ON TOBOGGANS, and even on the shoulders of their skiing handlers.

Oily, water-resistant fur tends to keep the snow from CLINGING AND CLUMPING on avalanche dogs such as Saint Bernards.

Despite modern technology, including helicopters, trained search and rescue dogs are still the FASTEST AT LOCATING PEOPLE TRAPPED UNDER SNOW.

DID THIS DOG FORGET ITS COAT? NO!

THE CHINESE CRESTED IS OFTEN HAIRLESS,

EXCEPT FOR TASSELS ON ITS HEAD, PAWS, AND TAIL.

THOUGHT TO HAVE ORIGINATED IN AFRICA, THIS ANCIENT BREED OFTEN SAILED ON CHINESE TRADING SHIPS TO HELP CATCH RATS.

QUIZ TIME

BONE UP ON YOUR CANINE COMPREHENSION. WRITE YOUR ANSWERS ON A SEPARATE PIECE OF PAPER AND CHECK THE ANSWER KEY BELOW. IF YOU'RE STUMPED, LOOK BACK THROUGH THE FIRST HALF OF THE BOOK.

1. What part of the dog is its muzzle?

    a. hind leg

    b. shoulder

    c. nose and mouth

    d. front paw

2. How long have dogs been around humans?

    a. 200 years

    b. 1,000 years

    c. 10 years

    d. over 14,000 years

3. Why do dogs bury bones?

    a. It's a game for them.

    b. They are saving them for when food is scarce.

    c. No one knows.

    d. They want to keep them away from cats.

4. Which dog is from the continent of Africa?

    a. Azawakh

    b. poodle

    c. German shepherd

    d. Newfoundland

5. True or False?

Dogs can usually recognize their reflection in a mirror.

6. Which dog was bred by the Chukchi people to pull sleds?

    a. bichon frise

    b. pug

    c. Siberian husky

    d. Chinese crested

7. Which dog breed is the smallest?

a. mastiff

b. Chihuahua

c. West Highland white terrier

d. basset hound

8. True or False?

Dogs can hear higher-pitched sounds than humans can.

9. Dogs are part of which scientific family?

a. Hominidae

b. Felidae

c. Canidae

d. Anatidae

10. Which dog has the longest tail?

a. Irish wolfhound

b. Australian stumpy tail cattle dog

c. Pembroke Welsh corgi

d. French bulldog

11. How many teeth do dogs have?

a. 10

b. 32

c. 42

d. 109

12. True or False?

Some dogs can smell people trapped under 20 feet (6.1 m) of snow.

GOING FOR GOLD

HUMANS AREN'T THE ONLY ANIMALS THAT COMPETE IN SPORTS. MEET SOME DOGLYMPIANS.

THE FRISBEE CATCH

How many of these discs can you catch in three minutes? One dog caught 20—enough to beat the previous world record of 16! Amazingly, this dog was afraid of them when it was a puppy. With practice, it overcame its fear and became a champion!

THE 100-METER DASH

Greyhounds are the fastest dogs. In long-distance running, a greyhound can outlast a cheetah. But when it comes to the zany game of running a 100-meter (109-yard) dash with a can on top of your head, the record belongs to a border collie/Australian shepherd mix. The dog ran it in under three minutes

CHERIE

HANGING TEN

Some hounds like to "hang ten" just like humans do. Cherie, a French bulldog, has won many awards in surfing contests. In 2019, she took first place at a Pacifica, California, U.S.A., surfing contest. Of course, even though dogs are good swimmers, these sea dogs wear life jackets for safety.

THE HIGH JUMP

The record for the highest jump, 68 inches (1.7 m) was held by a greyhound named Cinderella May. But in 2017, another greyhound shattered the record by leaping to a height of 75.5 inches (1.9 m). That's more than six feet (1.8 m), which is the height of a tall adult man.

TENNIS

Large or small, dogs love to chase and catch tennis balls. But a golden retriever holds the world record for holding the most tennis balls in its mouth at one time. How many did it hold? Six!

HOWLS AND GROWLS

LIKE WOLVES, SOME DOGS HOWL. WOLF HOWLS CAN BE HEARD UP TO 10 MILES (16 KM) AWAY IN OPEN AREAS.

The BASENJI, an African breed, never barks. But it's not silent—it makes sounds like YODELS AND WHINES.

Grrrrr.
Except when playing tug-of-war, a dog growl is a warning.

Some dogs sing along with a piano. But NEW GUINEA SINGING DOGS sing a cappella, or without music. Sometimes they sing together like a chorus!

SOME DOGS MAY EVEN BE ABLE TO COPY HUMAN SPEECH, ESPECIALLY PHRASES LIKE "I LOVE YOU."

A dog's howl can mean:
"I'M ALONE AND WANT SOME ATTENTION."
But some dogs howl just for fun.

Some dogs have been known to bark really fast—up to **90 times a minute** or more. *Woof, woof!*

A DOG'S SIGH WHEN CURLING UP TO SLEEP IS A SIGN OF HAPPINESS.

AFTER THEY DOZE OFF, SOME DOGS SNORE!

YAPPY YUMMIES

IF YOU DON'T HAVE A DOG TO SHARE THESE WITH, ASK AN ADULT IF YOU CAN TRY THEM YOURSELF—THEY'RE SAFE TO EAT! OR CALL YOUR LOCAL ANIMAL SHELTER OR RESCUE ORGANIZATION AND ASK IF THEY ACCEPT HOMEMADE TREATS AS DONATIONS.

Dogs love treats. Just like you might prefer ice cream over vegetables, dogs like to be spoiled, too. It gets boring eating kibble every day! Most dogs will do anything for a morsel of delicious food. This makes treats a valuable way to train and reward dogs. Protein-filled goodies with a strong smell are the key to most dogs' tummies. Try these homemade cheese and bacon dog cookies that are so good you might want to eat them, too!

YOU WILL NEED:

AN ADULT TO HELP

2 CUPS (322 G) ALL-PURPOSE FLOUR

1 CUP (100 G) SHREDDED CHEESE

1/2 CUP (60 G) CRUMBLED BACON (OPTIONAL)

2/3 CUP (160 ML) WATER

2 TABLESPOONS (30 ML) VEGETABLE OIL

BOWL

ROLLING PIN OR A TALL DRINKING GLASS

SMALL COOKIE CUTTER (ANY SHAPE WILL WORK, BUT A BONE WILL BE THE MOST FUN!)

COOKIE SHEET

OVEN FOR BAKING

PARCHMENT PAPER (OPTIONAL)

STEP 1:

Mix the flour, cheese, and bacon in a bowl. Stir in the water and oil, and then knead with your hands to make a firm dough.

MAKE SURE AN ADULT IS ON HAND TO SUPERVISE OR HELP YOU OUT!

STEP 2:

Roll the dough between two sheets of parchment paper or on a floured surface with a rolling pin or the side of a tall drinking glass until it's about 1/2 inch (1.25 cm) thick. Remove the parchment paper and then have an adult help you use the cookie cutter to press out cookies. Lay the cookies on a cookie sheet.

STEP 3:

Ask an adult to preheat the oven to 350 degrees F (175°C). Then bake the cookies for about 30 minutes until they are completely dry. Larger cookies will take longer. After the cookies cool, store them in an airtight container in the refrigerator. Use them within one week or freeze for later.

IF YOU WANT TO EAT THESE TREATS BUT YOU HAVE DIETARY RESTRICTIONS, FEEL FREE TO SUBSTITUTE INGREDIENTS SUCH AS TURKEY BACON OR GLUTEN-FREE FLOUR.

CANINE COMEDY

Q What's a dog's favorite snack at the movies?

A Pupcorn.

Q Why did the Dalmatian hide in a puddle of white paint?

A To avoid being spotted.

TONGUE TWISTER

SAY THIS FAST THREE TIMES:

Polly the poodle piddled in a puddle.

SOFIA: What do you get if you cross a frog and a dog?

HAKEEM: I don't know. What?

SOFIA: A croaker spaniel.

RIDDLE ME THIS...

Q Two dogs are sitting together. One is red and the other is spotted. The spotted dog is the red dog's son, but the red dog is not the spotted dog's father. Why?

A The red dog is the spotted dog's mother.

Q What do you do when a Chihuahua sneezes?

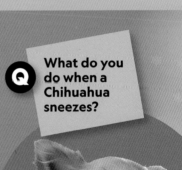

A Give it a tiny tissue.

Q What do you call a magical dog?

A A Labracadabrador.

K-9 LIE DETECTORS

Have you ever tried to trick a dog? Maybe you pretended to have a cookie in your hand to get the dog to follow you. Or maybe you said you were going for a walk when you were really going to the vet! A little white lie seems like a good way to get a dog's cooperation. After all, they don't know you're lying, right? Wrong! Scientists have discovered that dogs may know when people can't be trusted.

PICK A BUCKET

To explore whether dogs can detect lies, scientists used two buckets. First, dogs watched someone hide a piece of food in one bucket. Then, before the dogs could collect the food, someone else entered the room and encouraged them to pick the empty bucket by pointing to it. Sometimes the person pointing watched the food being hidden and knew the bucket they suggested was empty. Other times they were

out of the room when the food was hidden and believed they were pointing at the full bucket. So, sometimes they were lying on purpose, but other times they were simply mistaken.

A MISTAKE OR A LIE?

The scientists wondered if the dogs would follow the pointer's suggestion or believe their own eyes. When the pointer was only mistaken, many dogs trusted the pointer's advice even though they had seen the food being placed in the other bucket. When the pointer was lying on purpose, most of the dogs ignored them!

Believe it or not, apes and children under five follow the pointer's suggestion, even when the pointer is lying. Wow! Dogs can do something even young kids can't. Perhaps after living with humans for thousands of years, dogs have developed the ability to read our minds and judge whether we're trustworthy.

THE TERRIERS
IN THE EXPERIMENT
TRUSTED THE
POINTER'S LIE MORE
THAN ANY OF THE
OTHER BREEDS.

WHERE DO DOGS COME FROM?

IT'S HARD TO IMAGINE A WORLD WITHOUT DOGS.

It was only some 14,000 to 40,000 years ago that dogs evolved. But where did they come from? You guessed it—wolves! Today's gray wolves and our favorite pets share a common wolf ancestor. So, what led to that split in the family tree? Why did dogs come to be? Scientists aren't exactly sure, but here are two likely explanations.

THEORY 1: PET WOLVES

Just as we love to keep pets today, early humans might have wanted animal companions, too. And what's cuter than a baby wolf? Some scientists believe people caught wild wolf pups and raised them as pets. But they would only have kept the tame ones—wild animals that learned to be comfortable around humans. The ones that were too aggressive would have been released back into the wild. People would have kept the friendlier ones until they were fully grown. Then when those adult wolves had pups of their own, the process repeated—only the tamer pups were kept. Over many generations, the pet wolves that remained would have become friendlier and friendlier, until eventually they became domesticated,

that is an animal that is born comfortable around people. These domesticated wolves were early dogs.

THEORY 2: HUNGRY SCAVENGERS

Another possibility is that wolves domesticated themselves! Early humans' garbage would have provided wolves with an easy food source of bones, meat scraps, and poop. While many wolves would have been too scared to approach human camps, others would have bravely scavenged the garbage. Over time, this would have led to two groups of wolves—the wild ones that avoided people and the friendly ones that hung around for meals. If the scavenging wolves only bred with each other, over time they would have had friendlier and friendlier pups. These pups eventually became dogs.

WHAT DO YOU THINK?

Which explanation makes more sense to you? Can you imagine keeping a wild wolf as a pet? That could get messy! Or do you think living around humans can change an animal's personality? (Consider city-dwelling raccoons!) Whatever the cause, it's certain that without humans, we wouldn't have dogs.

THE FIRST DOGS WOULD HAVE BEEN USEFUL TO EARLY HUMANS AS HUNTING HELPERS, GUARDS, AND COMPANIONS.

WHAT DOG-RELATED JOB IS RIGHT FOR YOU?

I f you can't get enough of dogs, maybe you need a career in the dog world. But what dog-related job is right for you? To find out, answer these questions. Pick the answer that best matches your feelings, but choose only one answer for each question. Write down the letter of each answer on a piece of paper.

1. Your friend wants to go for a hike. You _____.

a. find the right clothes and hat

b. fetch a first aid kit

c. share your best hiking tips

d. jump up and down—you love to hike

e. suggest a movie instead

2. You are invited to a party. You _____.

a. pull out your fanciest clothes

b. take your temperature to make sure you won't spread any germs

c. practice your dance moves

d. race over early

e. snuggle your dog before you go

3. Your friend asks you to babysit her hamster. You _____.

a. can't wait to pet its soft fur

b. ask them what to do in case of an emergency

c. research tricks you can teach the hamster

d. power walk over to her house

e. debate whether to bring your dog along

4. What is your favorite subject in school?

a. art

b. science

c. quiet reading time

d. after-school sports

e. any classes with your friends

5. If you could live anywhere, where would you live?

a. Paris, the fashion capital of the world

b. somewhere with lots of museums

c. somewhere with your own obstacle course

d. the great outdoors

e. anywhere you can take your dog

6. Which activity do you prefer?

b. drawing

c. reading a book

d. helping a younger student

e. hiking

f. playing with my dog

7. What is your favorite type of weather?

a. You like when it's rainy outside.

b. You like to stay inside.

c. You love a sunny day.

d. You don't let the weather stop you!

e. You like a little bit of everything.

Check your score. Count up how many of each letter you have chosen. Then read the results below. If you have a tie score, read the results for both letters:

Three or more a's:
The scissors are calling—you should be a dog groomer! You like personal grooming, so why not train and get a certificate to groom dogs? Brushing and taking care of a dog's coat shows a dog that you care. And dog baths? Well, not all dogs are fans, but afterward, they always feel better.

Three or more b's:
Get out the white coat—you would make a great veterinarian. Vets are the doctors of the animal world, and they diagnose and treat sick and injured animals, including dogs. To become a vet, study hard because you will need to get a doctor of veterinary medicine degree.

Three or more c's:
Sit. Stay. Consider being a dog trainer. Training dogs teaches them how to behave around humans and other dogs and helps them when they feel anxious. You can even become certified as a dog trainer. But dog trainers don't just train dogs—they can also teach people how to be good owners and to understand their dogs.

Three or more d's:
Warm up your legs—you would make an excellent dog walker. Dog walkers perform a valuable service. They help people who can't be home with their pets all the time. Many dog walkers take animal care courses, or even get certified.

Three or more e's (or not three or more of anything):
You are a dog lover! And is there anything better than that? Not to a dog! Owning a doggy daycare and grooming salon where you can play with pooches all day long might be just the career for you.

HOUND HUMOR

KNOCK, KNOCK.

Who's there?
Bone.
Bone who?
Bone appetite!
It's dinnertime.

Q Where do dogs practice for a driving test?

A The barking lot.

Q What do you call a dog that runs a hot dog stand?

A A wiener dog.

TONGUE TWISTER

SAY THIS FAST THREE TIMES:

Boisterous beagles bake bunches of bagels by the beach.

DOG 1: Can you tell time?

DOG 2: Absolutely! I'm a watch dog.

RIDDLE ME THIS...

Q

Why is the bloodhound an excellent tour guide?

A He nose his way around!

KYRA: How do you stop a dog from digging in the backyard?

AESHA: I don't know. How?

KYRA: Put her in the front yard!

73

SUPER SPEED

If you've ever seen a dog chase a squirrel, you know how fast dogs can be. Even tiny breeds can motor! Some breeds are super at sprinting over short distances, while others are built for going the distance. The fastest dogs are those with lean bodies, deep chests, and long legs. Check out how fast some dogs have been known to run.

GREYHOUND
TOP SPEED:
42.5 mph
(68.4 km/h)

WHIPPET
TOP SPEED:
41 mph
(65.98 km/h)

BORZOI
TOP SPEED:
38.6 mph
(62.1 km/h)

MOST DOGS LEAVE US IN THE DUST. THE FASTEST SPEED OF ANY HUMAN IS 27.3 MILES AN HOUR (44 KM/H).

MIXED BREED
TOP SPEED:
35.5 mph
(57.1 km/h)

YORKSHIRE TERRIER
TOP SPEED:
20 mph
(32.7 km/h)

HOUNDS OF HISTORY

ΕΛΛΑΣ - HELLAS Λ.30

ALONG WITH PEOPLE, THE ANCIENT EGYPTIANS AND THE CHIRIBAYA PEOPLE OF ANCIENT PERU **MUMMIFIED THEIR BELOVED DOGS** THAT HAD DIED AND BURIED THEM WITH BLANKETS AND FOOD FOR THE AFTERLIFE.

In ancient Greek mythology, Cerberus was a **multiheaded dog** that guarded the underworld to keep spirits from leaving.

In the northwest part of North America, Indigenous people used the fur of a now extinct breed of **fluffy white dog,** called the Salish woolly dog, to make blankets.

FOR THOUSANDS OF YEARS, PEOPLE HAVE CELEBRATED THE **KUKUR TIHAR FESTIVAL IN NEPAL** AS "DOG DAY." CANINES ARE HONORED WITH FOOD, FLOWERS, AND A **RED TIKA MARK** ON THEIR FOREHEADS.

ONE FAMOUS MOVIE CHARACTER, **RIN TIN TIN,** WAS PLAYED BY A GERMAN SHEPHERD THAT WAS RESCUED AS A PUPPY. AN AMERICAN SERVICEMAN FOUND HIM IN FRANCE DURING WORLD WAR I.

During World War I, **Sergeant Stubby,** a bull terrier mix, supposedly warned American soldiers of enemy gas attacks so they could put on protective masks.

Greyfriars Bobby is a bronze statue in Edinburgh, Scotland, honoring a Skye terrier named Bobby that guarded his owner's grave for 14 years. Some people rub the statue's nose for luck.

CREATED THOUSANDS OF YEARS AGO, THE CHINESE ZODIAC REPRESENTS EACH YEAR USING ONE OF **12 ANIMALS.** THE YEAR **2030** WILL BE THE **YEAR OF THE DOG.**

EACH YEAR SINCE 2001, THE CANNES FILM FESTIVAL IN FRANCE HAS GIVEN OUT THE PALM DOG AWARD FOR DOGS IN FILMS. THE AWARD IS A DOG COLLAR WITH THE WORDS PALM DOG, USUALLY IN GOLD.

POOCH PARTS

Can you tell which part of a dog is shown in these pictures? Write your guesses on a separate piece of paper and compare them to the answers on page 79.

1

2

3

4

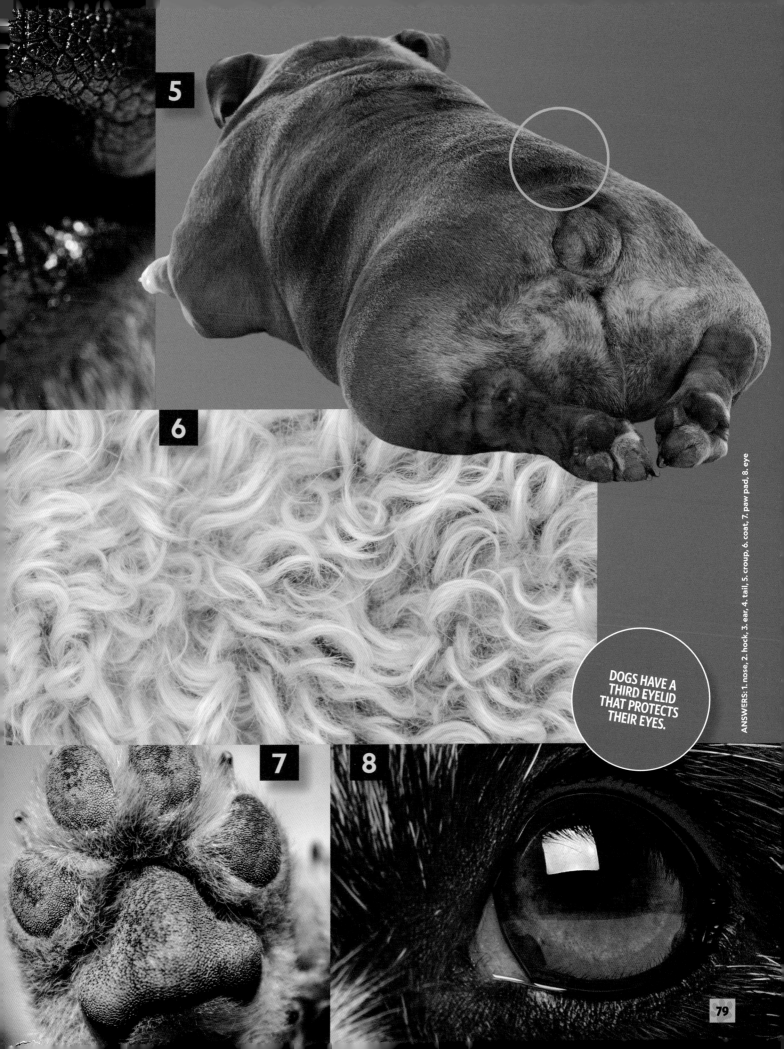

5

6

7

8

DOGS HAVE A THIRD EYELID THAT PROTECTS THEIR EYES.

ANSWERS: 1. nose, 2. hock, 3. ear, 4. tail, 5. croup, 6. coat, 7. paw pad, 8. eye

79

THROUGH THE EYES OF A DOG

SCIENTISTS THINK DOGS CAN SEE WITH ONLY ONE-FIFTH OF THE LIGHT HUMANS NEED.

CHOOSE BLUE TOYS FOR PLAYING FETCH SO THEY STAND OUT FOR YOUR DOG.

Human view

Dog view

Human view

Dog view

DO DOGS SEE IN BLACK AND WHITE?

That was a popular belief for many years. But it's nonsense! Dogs absolutely see in color. They don't see colors the same way you do, though. Instead of seeing a bright rainbow of shades, dogs only see shades of yellow and blue, so their world is more muted. Why can't they see like you do? Get a peek inside a dog's eye.

RODS AND CONES

Dogs' eyes are a lot like yours. Millions of special cells called photoreceptors line the back of the eyeball. Their job is to absorb light and then send a signal to the brain about what they see. Some photoreceptors, known as rods, work well in low light and are great at seeing movement. But they see in shades of gray. The other photoreceptors are called cones, and they are responsible for seeing colors. While you have more cones than rods, dogs have way more rods than cones. This means they see movement much better than we do and can see well in dim light. Plus, while humans have three types of cones (one "sees" red, one "sees" green, and one "sees" blue), dogs only have two.

YELLOW AND BLUE WORLD

A dog's two types of cones see yellow and blue. They can't detect red or green. And this mutes their rainbow. It's like red-green color blindness in humans. But red and green objects aren't invisible—they simply overlap with other colors. So red, green, and yellow all look yellow to a dog! No wonder a dog can lose a red ball in the green grass.

WHEN A DOG IS AFRAID,

IT SOMETIMES CROUCHES OR
ROLLS ON ITS BACK.

THE DOG IS BEING SUBMISSIVE.

WHEN A DOG LIES ON ITS BACK, AND ITS TAIL, HEAD, AND LEGS
ARE RELAXED AND FLOPPY,

IT'S SAYING IT WANTS

A BELLY RUB.

SCIENTISTS THINK BELLY RUBS

FEEL GOOD TO DOGS!

SUBMISSIVE MEANS **ACCEPTING** THAT ANOTHER
PERSON OR ANIMAL IS **IN CHARGE.**

DOGS DEFEND
THE ENVIRONMENT

A GOOD CONSERVATION DOG IS HIGH ENERGY, SMART, AND INTENSELY FOCUSED SO THAT IT CAN WORK ALL DAY.

DOGS HAVE INCREDIBLE NOSES!

They use their sense of smell to help humans in so many ways. But did you know they also use their snouts to protect the environment? From bacteria in beehives to orca poop in the ocean, as long as something has an odor, a dog can find it. That's a useful skill for protecting wildlife. Take a sniff of all the things that conservation dogs can do.

SNIFF AND SEARCH

To save threatened or endangered species, scientists need to find them first. Traditional methods such as cameras, traps, and radio collars are far less effective than training a scent detection dog. Dogs can search for plants and animals in all kinds of harsh environments. Or they can find scat—a fancy term for animal poop! And the poop is valuable. Scientists use it to learn about an animal's diet and health. Conservation dogs can also search for animals that have died to help people monitor the harmful effects of human development.

GET OUT!

Dogs also help people who are working to stop invasive species. An invasive species is one that doesn't belong in a particular area and causes harm to that habitat. Dogs can search for these invaders so people can either remove them or prevent them from arriving in the first place. Another way that dogs help is in the fight against poaching—the illegal trapping and killing of animals. They can find the poachers to stop them in their tracks, sniff out their smuggled goods, or prevent them from hunting by helping authorities seize their weapons.

TO TRAIN A DOG TO FIND AN ODOR, PAIR THAT SMELL WITH A REWARD SUCH AS A TREAT OR A GAME OF FETCH.

CANINE COMEDY

Q What kind of dog washes its fur every day?

A A shampoodle.

Q Why did the dog fail dance class?

A It had two left feet.

Q What do dogs like for breakfast?

A Poached eggs.

TONGUE TWISTER

SAY THIS FAST THREE TIMES:

How many elk would an elk hound hound if an elk hound could hound elk?

LAUGHABLE LIST

A Dog's Favorite Desserts:

Pupcakes

Snickerpoodles

Pupsicles

DOG 1: I'm having a big party on Saturday.

DOG 2: Canine or ten of my friends come?

KNOCK, KNOCK.

Who's there? Interrupting otterhound. **Interrupting otter—** —Woof, woof!

Q What is Dracula's favorite dog?

A A bloodhound.

MANY-COLORED COATS

Dogs lose old fur, or shed, in different ways. Some **don't shed very much, but** others, such as the Great Pyrenees, **leave piles of fur on your floor.**

Brown dogs are called "chocolate." U.S. president Bill Clinton had a chocolate Labrador retriever named Buddy.

Some dogs, such as some spaniels and retrievers, sport a double coat. On the outside, they have WATER-PROOF GUARD HAIRS. Underneath, these dogs have woolly or fluffy fur.

Black Labrador retrievers can have yellow, black, or chocolate puppies—or one of each. Without genetic testing, an owner can't predict what the litter will look like.

THE PULI'S COAT **NATURALLY GROWS** IN CLUMPS OR MATS THAT LOOK LIKE THICK **STRINGS OR CORDS.**

Dalmatians are born **without spots.** Their spots show up in **large numbers** by the time they are around five months old.

DOG WHISKERS ARE STIFF HAIRS ON ITS FACE THAT HELP A DOG FEEL WHERE THINGS ARE.

A lozenge mark, usually on a dog's head, is known as a **"kissing spot."**

OCTOBER 1 IS **NATIONAL BLACK DOG DAY.**

Turn the page for more facts about colorful coats!

A dog's coat can be **silky, smooth, curly, rough, or even wiry.** **The wire fox terrier's coat protects it** from low, sharp plants when it is hunting.

When a show dog is not being groomed for a dog show, it usually gets a **"puppy cut"—** fluffy fur that is about the same length all over.

Shih Tzus often rock **ponytails** or topknots **tied with bows.**

Like humans, dogs tend to go gray when they get older— but only around the muzzle.

Dogs come in many colors. But very few breeds come in **only one particular solid color.** The Irish setter is all red and the Weimaraner is totally gray.

DOG GROOMERS
CAN GET PRETTY CREATIVE: SOMETIMES THEY USE **HARMLESS DYES** TO TURN A DOG'S FUR INTO A RAINBOW OF COLORS. (BUT DON'T TRY THIS AT HOME!)

POODLE HAIRCUTS
ARE DESIGNED TO HELP DOGS SWIM WHILE KEEPING THEIR CHESTS WARM. THE POMPOMS ON THEIR LEGS PROTECT THEIR JOINTS.

COAT MARKINGS
HAVE SPECIAL NAMES. A HARLEQUIN COAT HAS UNIQUELY SHAPED BLACK PATCHES ON WHITE FUR.

SOME DOGS, such as the Kerry blue terrier, have **COATS** that **DON'T BOTHER PEOPLE** with **ALLERGIES.**

TICKING means that a dog's coat has **LITTLE FLECKS** of **ANOTHER COLOR,** like freckles.

White markings on a dog's feet are called **"socks."**

HOUND HUMOR

KNOCK, KNOCK.

Who's there?
Dog.
Dog who?
Doggone it, are you ever going to let me in?

Q What do you call a dog wearing diamonds?

A A pampered pooch.

Q Why did the bulldog get a foul in the basketball game?

A Instead of dribbling, he drooled!

JAMAL: What do you name a dog that won't stay in the backyard?

TOM: I don't know. What?

JAMAL: Rover.

LAUGHABLE LIST

Musical Instruments for Dogs:

Xylabone

....

Trumpet

....

Howlmonica

....

Bagpups

....

RIDDLE ME THIS...

DOG 1: Where is your favorite place to shop?

DOG 2: The flea market.

Q How do dogs know who is prank calling them?

A Collar ID.

PUP MATCHUP

Puppies don't always look like the adult dogs they will grow into. Try matching the puppies above with the adult dogs below! On a separate piece of paper, write the numbers 1–8. Next to each number, write the letter of the adult dog that you think that puppy will grow into. Compare your answers to the answer key at the bottom of page 95.

1

2

3

ADULT DOGS

A

GERMAN SHEPHERD

B

PEMBROKE WELSH CORGI

C

PULI

D

LABRADOR RETRIEVER

4

5

6

7

8

E

IRISH SETTER

F

POODLE

G

DALMATIAN

H

YORKSHIRE TERRIER

CLEVER CANINES

BRIAN HARE, COMPARATIVE PSYCHOLOGIST

As a teenager, Brian did an experiment with his dog in his family's garage. He discovered that dogs have an amazing ability to read human gestures. Thanks to his breakthrough, scientists took a new interest in dog intelligence. Now Brian works as a comparative psychologist, which means he compares how different animals think and behave. By playing fun games with dogs in his lab, he hopes to find out how dogs' cognition—how their brains learn and understand the world—compares with that of humans and other animals.

WHAT LED TO YOUR INTEREST IN DOGS?

Like many dog owners, I spent countless hours playing fetch with my childhood dog, Oreo. If Oreo lost a ball, I'd help him find it by pointing in the right direction. Then, when I was 19 years old, my psychology professor told me that the ability to follow a pointing gesture might be unique to humans. I blurted out, "My dog can do that!" and it all began from there.

WHAT MAKES DOGS INTERESTING RESEARCH SUBJECTS?

Dogs have spread to all corners of the world, including inside our homes, and, in some cases, onto our beds. Most mammals have seen a sharp drop in their populations because of human activities. But there have never been more dogs on the planet than today. Dogs also have more jobs helping people than ever. We need to know how they think so we can help them do their jobs!

WHAT HAVE YOU LEARNED?

Because we keep them as pets, until recently science did not take the genius of dogs very seriously. People assumed dogs had lost the skills and intelligence needed to survive in the wild. Then I discovered that instead of being not so smart, our relationship with dogs gave them a special kind of intelligence. No other animal can read our gestures as well as dogs can. This allows them to be incredible partners with us, whether it's hunting, agility, or just everyday life. It also helps both dogs and people solve problems they can't solve on their own.

WHAT IS THE MOST EXCITING PART OF YOUR JOB?

The recent explosion in the field of dog cognition. Suddenly, all sorts of scientists have realized what has been under our noses the whole time—dogs are one of the most important species we can study. The intelligence of dogs is far more complicated and interesting than we thought possible.

WE HAVE LEARNED MORE ABOUT HOW DOGS THINK IN THE PAST 10 YEARS THAN WE LEARNED IN THE PAST 100.

IN THIS EXPERIMENT, SCIENTISTS OBSERVE WHETHER THE PUPPY CAN FIGURE OUT THAT SHE MUST ENTER THE CLEAR CYLINDER FROM THE SIDE TO GET THE TREAT—IF SHE APPROACHES HEAD-ON, SHE WILL BE BLOCKED BY THE BARRIER.

PUPPY POWER

THESE NUMBERS ARE FOR THE LARGEST RECORDED LITTER SIZE.

The only thing cuter than a puppy is a litter of puppies. The world record for the largest litter is held by a Neapolitan mastiff named Tia who gave birth to 24 puppies! Check out the litter sizes for several other breeds.

CHOW CHOW
Largest litter size: 9
Average litter size: about 4

PAPILLON
Largest litter size: 7
Average litter size: about 3

TOY POODLE
Largest litter size: 4
Average litter size: about 2

STANDARD SCHNAUZER
Largest litter size: 11
Average litter size: 7

BORDER COLLIE
Largest litter size: 16
Average litter size: 6

GOLDEN RETRIEVER
Largest litter size: 17
Average litter size: about 8

SAINT BERNARD
Largest litter size: 18
Average litter size: about 7

THE POWER OF PANTING

PANT, PANT, PANT! On a steamy summer day, you've probably seen dogs with their mouths hanging open and their tongues flopping out. Did you know they're trying to cool off in the hot weather? But we don't pant when we're hot! Instead, we cool off when sweat evaporates from our skin. Well, dogs don't sweat the way people do. In fact, the only sweat glands they have are between their paw pads. They need another way to stay cool. So how does panting work?

EVAPORATION SAVES THE DAY

As a dog pants, water from the inside of its mouth, breathing passages, and from the surface of its tongue evaporates. This means it goes from a liquid to a gas in the air. The evaporation cools the dog down from the inside out. The hotter the dog is, the faster it will pant. But panting isn't a great way to breathe, so every once in a while a dog must stop panting to get oxygen into its lungs.

MORE THAN FOR COOLING

Dogs also pant for other reasons. For example, they will pant when they are excited and playful or during heavy exercise. But sometimes panting is a warning signal. It can happen when a dog is stressed or in pain. It can also indicate a medical condition such as a heart problem or heatstroke. If a dog is panting more than normal or in an unusual situation, it's time to talk to an adult about calling the vet.

ALTHOUGH YOU WOULD THINK DOGS' FUR COATS WOULD MAKE THEM HOT IN THE SUMMER, THEY ACTUALLY PREVENT SUNBURN AND INSULATE DOGS FROM THE HOT WEATHER.

DOGS LOSE A LOT OF WATER FROM THEIR BODIES WHEN THEY PANT. THEY NEED ACCESS TO COOL, CLEAN WATER TO RECHARGE!

CANINE COMEDY

COLLIE: Want to get a pizza?
POODLE: Sure. What kind?
COLLIE: Puperoni.

PIZZA PIZZA
PIZZA PIZZA
PIZZA PIZZA

Q Why did the man in Iceland call his guard dog Frost?

A Because Frost bites.

Q What did the dog order at the coffee shop?

A A latte with whippet cream.

TONGUE TWISTER

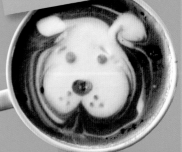

SAY THIS FAST THREE TIMES:
Pooped pups pooped.

RIDDLE ME THIS...

Q What's the difference between dogs and sheep?

A One has fleas and the other has fleece.

LAUGHABLE LIST

A Dog's Favorite Jobs:

Roofer
....
Pawthor
....
Barkeologist
....
Labrarian
....

Q What's the most popular game at a dog family picnic?

A Pug of war.

Q What's a dog's favorite rock song?

A "Bad to the Bone."

CANID COUSINS

In cartoons, **WILE E. COYOTE** was outsmarted by **ROADRUNNER.** In real life, coyotes don't snack on roadrunners often, but when they do, they have **NO TROUBLE CATCHING THEM!**

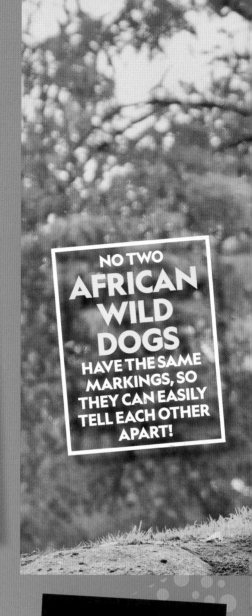

NO TWO **AFRICAN WILD DOGS** HAVE THE SAME MARKINGS, SO THEY CAN EASILY TELL EACH OTHER APART!

NORTH AMERICAN EXPLORERS LEWIS AND CLARK HAD NEVER SEEN COYOTES BEFORE. THEY CALLED THEM "PRAIRIE WOLVES."

Unlike their cousins, which are pack animals, **foxes like to live and hunt alone.**

DHOLES ARE WILD DOGS FOUND IN ASIA. They communicate through clucks and whistles.

AFRICAN WILD DOGS CAN SPRINT AT 44 MILES AN HOUR (71 KM/H).

Coyotes and wolves may be relatives, but if there's no other food source around, wolves have been known **to make a meal of a coyote.**

Jackals live mainly in Africa and come in three species: golden, side-striped, and black-backed.

MANY THOUSANDS OF DINGOES LIVE IN AUSTRALIA, WHERE THEY ARE CONSIDERED AN APEX PREDATOR— THE TOP OF THE FOOD CHAIN.

"DOG" AROUND THE WORLD

People all over the globe keep dogs as pets. But not everybody says "dog" the same way. Even in English, we have many words for dog—"pup," "doggo," and "pooch," to name just a few. Plus, humans speak more than 7,000 languages! That means there are a whole lot of words for our canine companions. This map shows the word for "dog" in seven different locations.

Word: *qimmiq (KIM-ick)*
Where: Northern Alaska
Language: Inupiaq

ARCTIC

Northern Alaska, U.S.A.

NORTH AMERICA

EUROPE

PACIFIC OCEAN

ATLANTIC OCEAN

BRAZIL
SOUTH AMERICA

Word: *cão*
(cow)
Where: Brazil
Language: Portuguese

Word: *mbwa (MM-bwa)*
Where: Kenya
Language: Swahili

AN

Word: *skýlos (SKI-lohs)*
Where: Greece
Language: Greek

Word: *sobaka (sah-BAH-ka)*
Where: Russia
Language: Russian

Word: *inu (IH-noo)*
Where: Japan
Language: Japanese

OCEAN

RUSSIA

ASIA

JAPAN

GREECE

INDIA

PACIFIC OCEAN

AFRICA

KENYA

INDIAN OCEAN

AUSTRALIA

SOUTHERN OCEAN

TARCTICA

Word: *kutta (kuh-TAH)*
Where: India
Language: Hindi

PAMPERED POOCHES

FOR SOME POOCHES, THERE'S NO LIMIT TO THE PAMPERING.

BLINGIEST

Dog owners sometimes buy rhinestone-studded collars for their canine companions. Some even adorn them in pooch pearls. But only a few can afford a dog collar made from real diamonds set in platinum. Price tag—more than $3 million!

FANCIEST BOWL

Some fancy dog bowls would be fit for a king or queen—even a human one! But it'd be hard to choose a favorite: Is it the 22-carat gold-plated porcelain dog bowl, or the sterling silver bowl from a world-famous jewelry company?

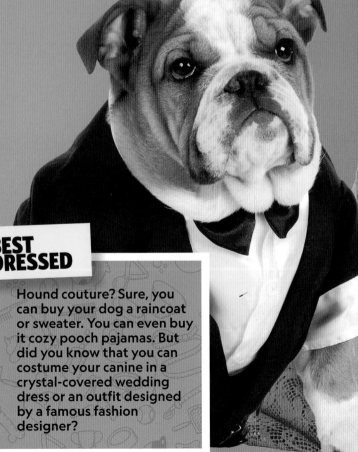

BEST DRESSED

Hound couture? Sure, you can buy your dog a raincoat or sweater. You can even buy it cozy pooch pajamas. But did you know that you can costume your canine in a crystal-covered wedding dress or an outfit designed by a famous fashion designer?

BIGGEST MANSION

"In the doghouse" can mean that you're in trouble. But not when the doghouse is lined with fine linen and covered in embroidered silk. Or when it's the biggest house on the block, with two dog-size bedrooms, a TV, and an automatic kibble dispenser.

SWEETEST SMELLING

Wet dogs smell like, well, wet dogs. Some people who want to sweeten their pooch's fragrance try some dog cologne. People can spritz or mist their pups with a fragrance created to be safe on dogs. There is even a specially made Fido "perfume" that can cost up to $4,000.

MORE EXPENSIVE DOESN'T ALWAYS MEAN BETTER—MOST DOGS ARE PERFECTLY HAPPY WITH A WARM BED, FOOD AND WATER, SHELTER, AND LOVE!

AT YOUR SERVICE

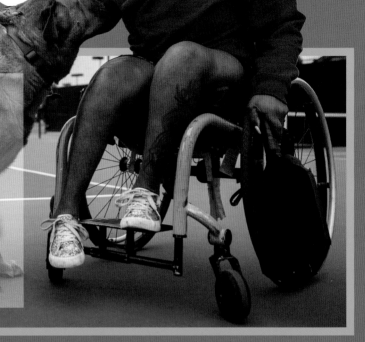

Service dogs
are trained to help owners who have certain disabilities. They are not the same as **working dogs** that help police and other professionals.

WHICH DOGS MAKE THE BEST SERVICE DOGS?
Calm, intelligent dogs, like Portuguese water dogs, Labrador retrievers, and Bernese mountain dogs.

Dogs have been known to act as guide dogs to other dogs that are **blind!**

THERAPY DOGS
VISIT AND COMFORT PEOPLE IN HOSPITALS AND RETIREMENT HOMES.

Owners who have trouble hearing are helped by HEARING ALERT DOGS that let them know when someone is calling or at the door.

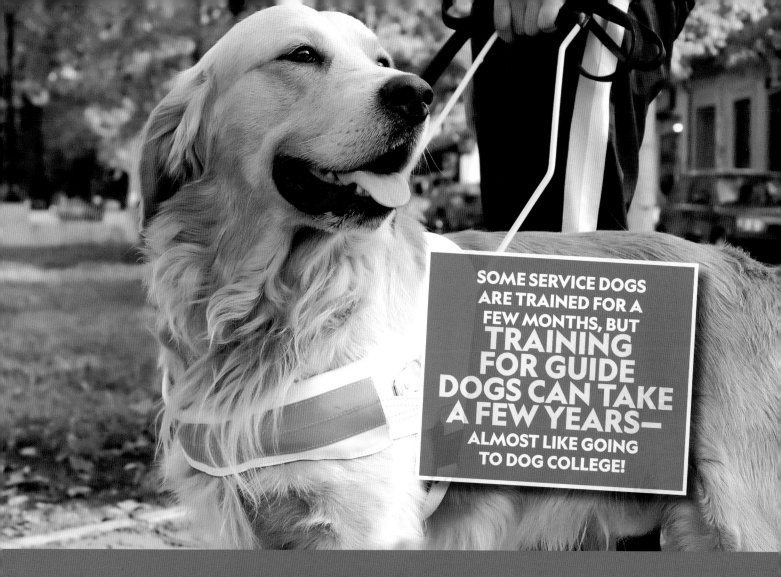

SOME SERVICE DOGS ARE TRAINED FOR A FEW MONTHS, BUT **TRAINING FOR GUIDE DOGS CAN TAKE A FEW YEARS—** ALMOST LIKE GOING TO DOG COLLEGE!

During the September 11, 2001, attack on the World Trade Center in New York City, a guide dog named Roselle helped her sight-impaired owner walk down 78 flights of stairs to safety.

AN ALLERGY ALERT DOG sniffs its owner's food—without eating it—and lets its owner know if the food contains something the owner is highly allergic to.

DON'T SMELL ANYTHING? A diabetic alert dog might. These dogs can smell when their owner's blood sugar is too high or too low.

Mobility assistant dogs help people who have trouble getting around by opening doors and fetching keys.

DO DOGS DREAM?

DOGS USUALLY START DREAMING AFTER THEY HAVE BEEN ASLEEP FOR 20 MINUTES.

BIG DOGS DREAM LESS OFTEN THAN SMALL DOGS, BUT THEIR DREAMS LAST LONGER.

HAVE YOU EVER WATCHED A DOG SLEEP?

You might have seen a twitching tail or paddling paws. Maybe you heard a whimper or growl. What's going on? Do dogs dream like you do? Yes! Scientists have studied brain activity in sleeping animals such as rats, cats, and dogs, and they found that what happens in these animals' sleep looks a lot like what happens when they're awake. Find out when dogs dream and how you can recognize it.

REM RULES!

When we sleep, our bodies go through different stages. One stage is known as REM sleep, which stands for rapid eye movement. When we're in REM sleep, our bodies are very relaxed, but our brains are busy. This is the stage when we do most of our dreaming. And guess what? Dogs have REM sleep, too. So, if you want to catch a dog dreaming, look for signs of REM. Its breathing will become shallow and less regular. But the big giveaway will be its eyes. Its eyelids may flicker, and underneath the lids, its eyes will quickly move back and forth as if it's watching a tennis match. Let the dreams begin!

THE STUFF OF DREAMS

Do dogs dream about fun and games, like chasing squirrels or playing fetch? Nobody knows for sure. But a study with rats showed they had the exact same brain activity when they were dreaming as they did when they were running a maze earlier in the day. So, it's likely dogs dream about their usual activities, too. And that might include activities they don't enjoy, such as having a bath. If a dog seems upset in its sleep, it may be having a nightmare. But just let it sleep. A dog might act out if you wake it when it's frightened.

HOUND HUMOR

Q Where do scientists study dog behavior?

A The laboratory.

Q What did the sled dog driver say to his team of Siberian huskies?

A Thank you very mush.

114

JANET: When should you walk your dog?

AZUMI: I don't know. When?

JANET: When they leash expect it!

RIDDLE ME THIS...

Q How do you call a dog without making a sound?

FWEET!

A A dog whistle.

TONGUE TWISTER

SAY THIS FAST THREE TIMES:
The hounds bow down in leaps and bounds without a sound.

PAW PRINT PICASSO

Would you like to make some pawsitively pupperific art? With just a few supplies, you can create your own paw print painting. First, mold the most realistic paws you can, and then use paint to stamp prints across the page. Let your paw prints tell a story. Will you have two dogs playing together? Or maybe one dog chasing its tail? Let your paws do the painting and create a masterpiece!

YOU WILL NEED:
MODELING CLAY OR HOUSEHOLD OBJECTS YOU CAN SHAPE INTO PAWS
NONTOXIC WASHABLE PAINT
COOKIE SHEET OR LARGE PLATE
LARGE PIECE OF PAPER OR CANVAS

STEP 1:
Using the diagram of a front and back paw, mold your own dog paws. You can use clay for the entire paw or make a separate clay stamp for each type of paw pad (see step 2). You can also use household objects such as marshmallows molded into the right shapes with toothpicks for claws. You can even ask an adult to help you carve a potato print paw stamp.

MAKE YOUR PAW STAMPS AS REALISTIC AS POSSIBLE BY MODELING THEM AFTER YOUR OWN DOG'S FEET. YOU CAN GET A GOOD LOOK WITH THE "SHAKE A PAW" TRICK. OR, IF YOU DON'T WANT TO DISTURB YOUR PAL, LOOK AT YOUR PUP'S PAWS WHILE HE'S SLEEPING. YOU CAN ALSO HAVE AN ADULT HELP YOU STUDY PHOTOS OF DOG PAWS ON THE INTERNET.

STEP 2:

Don't forget that the front and back paws look different. Both have four toe pads called digital pads. But the front paw has a heart-shaped metacarpal pad while the back paw has a rounder metatarsal pad. All front paws have dewclaws, but they are missing from the back feet of many dogs. And finally, the front paws have a carpal pad higher up the leg. This pad only touches the ground when the dog is braking, making swift turns, or climbing steep hills.

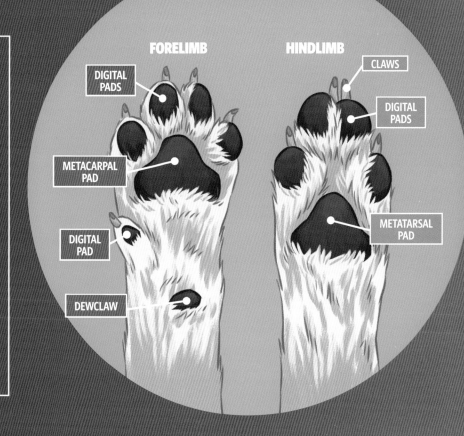

FORELIMB   HINDLIMB

DIGITAL PADS
CLAWS
DIGITAL PADS
METACARPAL PAD
DIGITAL PAD
METATARSAL PAD
DEWCLAW

LOOK FOR EARTH-FRIENDLY WAYS TO RECYCLE OBJECTS INTO PAW STAMPS. FOR EXAMPLE, ASK AN ADULT TO HELP YOU CUT A USED (BUT CLEAN!) KITCHEN SPONGE INTO PAW PAD SHAPES. OR, IF YOU'VE HAD A PACKAGE DELIVERED, TRY STAMPING WITH THE PACKING PEANUTS OR PIECES OF PACKING FOAM.

STEP 3:

Once your front and back paws are complete, spread a thin layer of paint over the cookie sheet or plate. Use this as a stamp pad for your paws. Press them into the paint, then press them onto your paper to make prints. Make as many paw prints as you need to tell your story. Use different colors of paint to show different dogs or to simply have fun.

BECAUSE OF A DOG'S ANAL GLANDS, EVERY MUTT'S BUTT SMELLS DIFFERENT.

HEY OLD FRIEND, GOOD TO SMELL YOU AGAIN!

THE JACOBSON'S ORGAN IN A DOG'S NOSE HELPS THE DOG DIFFERENTIATE SMELLS, SO A BUTT SNIFF IS NOT CONFUSED BY ANY LINGERING WHIFF OF POOP.

QUIZ TIME

BONE UP ON YOUR CANINE COMPREHENSION. WRITE YOUR ANSWERS ON A SEPARATE PIECE OF PAPER AND CHECK THE ANSWERS BELOW. IF YOU'RE STUMPED, LOOK BACK THROUGH THE SECOND HALF OF THE BOOK.

1 What is the record for the most tennis balls held in a dog's mouth at one time?

a. 2

b. 6

c. 10

d. 20

2 True or False?

Many dogs can tell if a person is lying.

3 What does a veterinarian do?

a. plays games

b. serves in the military

c. takes care of animals

d. cooks hamburgers

4 True or False?

Dogs only see in black and white.

5 How can dogs help in conservation efforts?

a. poop less

b. search for bacteria in beehives

c. play more Frisbee

d. be nice to cats

6 What are the white markings on a dog's feet called?

a. pajamas

b. berets

c. slippers

d. socks

7 The record for the most puppies in a litter is _____.

a. 3

b. 9

c. 24

d. 100

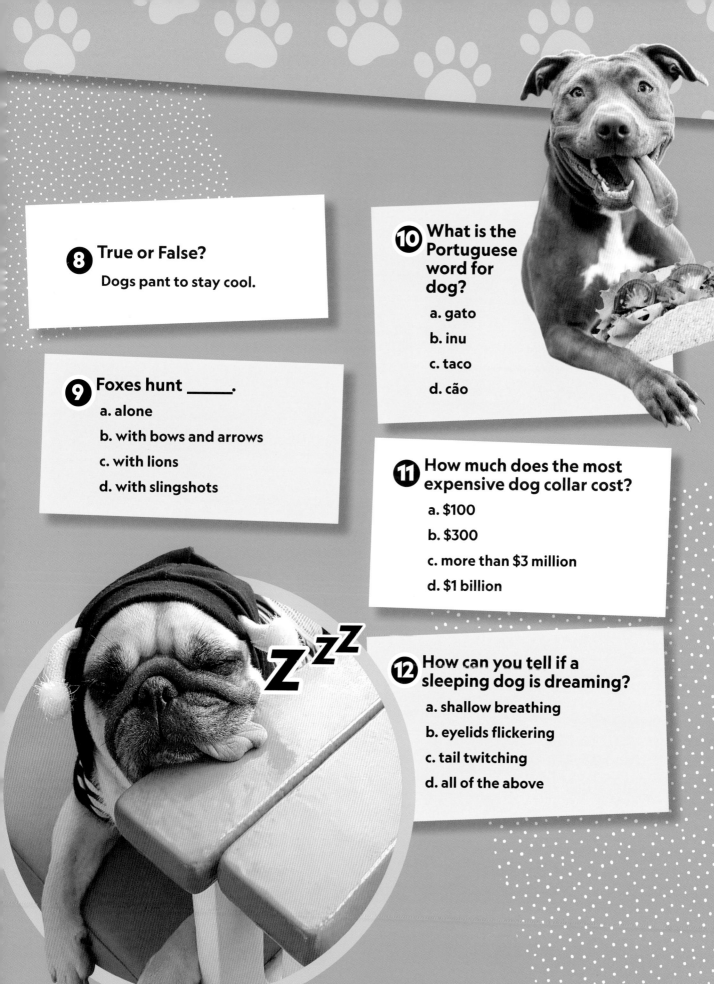

8 **True or False?**

Dogs pant to stay cool.

9 Foxes hunt _____.

a. alone

b. with bows and arrows

c. with lions

d. with slingshots

10 **What is the Portuguese word for dog?**

a. gato

b. inu

c. taco

d. cão

11 **How much does the most expensive dog collar cost?**

a. $100

b. $300

c. more than $3 million

d. $1 billion

12 **How can you tell if a sleeping dog is dreaming?**

a. shallow breathing

b. eyelids flickering

c. tail twitching

d. all of the above

Z Z Z

BREED PRONUNCIATION GUIDE

HERE'S HOW TO PRONOUNCE THE DOG BREEDS IN THIS BOOK.

A

Akita: a-KEE-ta
Alaskan malamute: uh-LASK-in MAL-uh-mewt
Australian cattle dog: aw-STRAIL-yun CAT-tul dog
Azawakh: AH-za-wahk

B

Basset hound: BASS-it hound
Beagle: BEE-gull
Bedlington terrier: BED-ling-tun TARE-ee-ur
Bernese mountain dog: bur-NEEZ MOWN-tin dog
Bloodhound: BLUD-hound
Border collie: BOR-der CAH-lee
Borzoi: BORE-zoy
Boxer: BOX-er

C

Catahoula leopard dog: CAT-a-HOO-la LEP-ard dog
Chihuahua: chee-WAH-wah
Coton de Tulear: KO-tone Dih TOO-lee-ARE

D

Dalmatian: dal-MAY-shun
Dandie Dinmont: DAN-dee DIN-mont
Dogue de Bordeaux: DOHG-day bore-DOE

G

Golden retriever: GOLD-in ri-TREE-ver
Great Dane: Great DAYNE
Great Pyrenees: Great PEER-eh-neez

K

Komondor: KAH-men-door

L

Labrador retriever: LAB-ruh-dore ri-TREE-ver
Lagotto Romagnolo: la-GOH-toe rome-ahn-YOH-lo
Lhasa Apso: LAH-sa AP-so

M

Mastiff: MAH-stiff
Molossus: mo-LAH-sus

N

Neapolitan mastiff: NEE-eh-PAH-luh-ten MAH-stiff
New Guinea singing dog: New GIH-nee singing dog
Newfoundland: NEW-fund-lend

P

Papillon: PA-pee-yawn
Pembroke Welsh corgi:
  PEM-brook WELSH KOR-gee
Peruvian Inca Orchid:
  pe-ROO-vee-an IN-ca OR-kid
Petit Basset Griffon Vendéen:
  puh-TEE bah-SAY gree-FOHN
  VON-day-uhn
Pomeranian: PAH-muh-RAY-nee-in
Poodle: POO-dull
Puli: PUH-lee

R

Rottweiler: ROTT-why-ler

S

Salish woolly dog: SAY-lish WOOL-ee dog
Saluki: sa-LOO-kee
Schnauzer: SCHNOW-zer
Shiba Inu: SHEE-ba EE-noo
Shih Tzu: SHEET-soo
Siberian husky: sigh-BEER-ee-an HUH-skee

W

Weimaraner: WHY-mer-EYE-ner
Whippet: WIP-it

Y

Yorkshire terrier:
  YORK-shur TARE-ee-ur

FIND OUT MORE

Adults, you can learn more about dogs with your child with these online resources:

American Kennel Club

Britannica

National Geographic Kids

INDEX

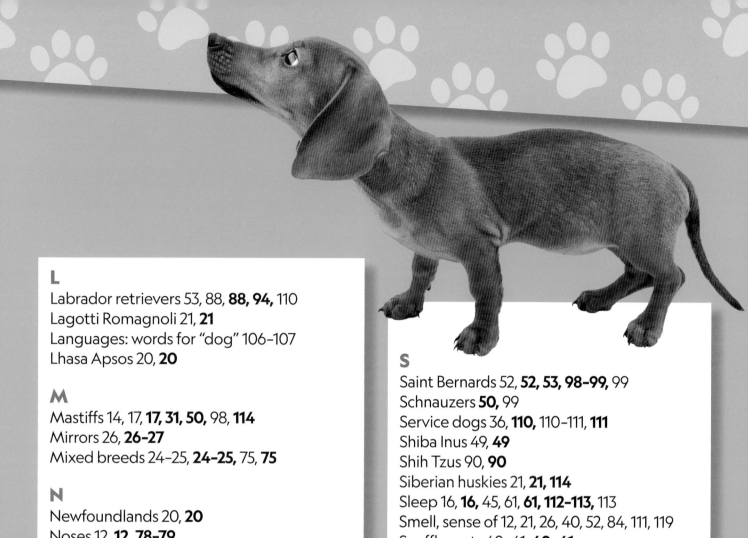

CREDITS

(LO LE), cynoclub/Adobe Stock; 66, PM Images/Getty Images; 67, manushot/Adobe Stock; 68–69, Kenton D. Gomez/Shutterstock; 70 (UP E), Reel2Reel/Shutterstock; 70 (LO CTR), chris_tina/Shutterstock; 70 (LO LE), olegganko/Shutterstock; 71 (UP), Azaliya (Elya Vatel)/Adobe Stock; 71 (A), Irina/Adobe Stock; 71 (B), didesign/Adobe Stock; 71 (C), leungchopan/Adobe Stock; 71 (D), luckybusiness/Adobe Stock; 71 (E), iwavephoto/Adobe Stock; 72 (UP), Erik Lam/Adobe Stock; 72 (LO RT), alexugalek/Adobe Stock; 72 (bagel), DenisMArt/Adobe Stock; 72 (dachshund), Artem/Adobe Stock; 72 (LO CTR), Stuart Monk/Shutterstock; 72 (LO LE), aerogondo/Adobe Stock; 73 (UP LE), Happy monkey/Adobe Stock; 73 (UP RT), nsc_photography/Adobe Stock; 73 (LO LE), majivecka/Adobe Stock; 74–75 (sky), Elenamiv/Shutterstock; 74–75 (grass), santagig/Adobe Stock; 74 (greyhound), R.Bitzer Photography/Adobe Stock; 74 (whippet), Ivan Berta/Shutterstock; 74–75 (borzoi), otsphoto/Adobe Stock; 75 (mixed), Yvonne/Adobe Stock; 75 (terrier), Ekaterina Kobalnova/Adobe Stock; 76 (UP RT), rook76/Adobe Stock; 76 (LE), chempina/Shutterstock; 76 (LO), Nadia/Adobe Stock; 77 (UP), Warner Bros./Photofest; 77 (CTR LE), Library of Congress Prints and Photographs Division; 77 (LO LE), Fred Dufour/Getty Images; 77 (LO RT), Pugun & Photo Studio/Adobe Stock; 78 (1), adogslifephoto/Adobe Stock; 78 (2), Lisa J. Goodman/Getty Images; 78 (3), Sir Francis Canker Photography/Getty Images; 78 (4), Panther Media GmbH/Alamy Stock Photo; 79 (5), Willee Cole/Adobe Stock; 79 (6), MXW Photography/Adobe Stock; 79 (7), Agapov Fedor/Adobe Stock; 79 (8), Erik Lam/Adobe Stock; 80–81, Fly_dragonfly/Adobe Stock; 81 (UP), Mariusz Blach/Adobe Stock; 81 (UP CTR), András Péter/DogVision; 81 (LO CTR), kellyvandellen/Adobe Stock; 81 (LO), András Péter/DogVision; 82–83, Cryber/Shutterstock; 84–85, Uwe Anspach/picture alliance via Getty Image; 85, Philipp von Ditfurth/dpa/Newscom; 86 (UP), jjwithers/Getty Images; 86 (LO RT), Colin/Adobe Stock; 86 (LO CTR), jordache/Shutterstock; 86 (woman), New Africa/Adobe Stock; 86 (LO LE), Artsilense/Shutterstock; 87 (UP LE), Rawpixel/Adobe Stock; 87 (UP CTR), Sandra/Adobe Stock; 87 (LO RT), lourdesphoto/Adobe Stock; 87 (LO LE), Kuznetsov Alexey/Shutterstock; 87 (cape), Bohdan Skrypnyk/Adobe Stock; 88 (UP), Nynke/Adobe Stock; 88 (LO), chrt2hrt/Adobe Stock; 89 (UP), Borina Olga/Shutterstock; 89 (LO RT), timaj69/Adobe Stock; 89 (LO LE), Dulova Olga/Shutterstock; 90 (UP LE), TSViPhoto/Adobe Stock; 90 (CTR RT), Eric Isselée/Adobe Stock; 90 (LO RT), Amelia/Adobe Stock; 90 (LO LE), Mikkel Bigandt/Adobe Stock; 90 (CTR LE), Happy monkey/Adobe Stock; 91 (UP), Igor Emmerich/Getty Images; 91 (CTR LE), Animal Photography/Alamy Stock Photo; 91 (LO LE), Studio Porto Sabbia/Adobe Stock; 91 (LO RT), VKarlov/Shutterstock; 92 (UP), truengtra/Adobe Stock; 92 (LO RT), Elia R/Adobe Stock; 92 (LO LE), adogslifephoto/Adobe Stock; 93 (UP),

brusnikaphoto/Adobe Stock; 93 (LO RT), helga1981/Adobe Stock; 93 (LO LE), Suraphol/Adobe Stock; 93 (flea), Amplion/Shutterstock; 94 (1), anetapics/Shutterstock; 94 (2), Intarapong/Shutterstock; 94 (3), vivienstock/Adobe Stock; 94 (A), Mikkel Bigandt/Adobe Stock; 94 (B), Zuz/Adobe Stock; 94 (C), sue/Adobe Stock; 94 (D), SasaStock/Adobe Stock; 95 (4), DeingeL_/Adobe Stock; 95 (5), Happy monkey/Adobe Stock; 95 (6), tsik/Shutterstock; 95 (7), Alexandra/Adobe Stock; 95 (8), Yulia/Adobe Stock; 95 (E), DragoNika/Adobe Stock; 95 (F), disq/Adobe Stock; 95 (G), Rita Kochmarjova/Adobe Stock; 95 (H), Birute Vijeikiene/Adobe Stock; 96, Vanessa Woods; 97 (ALL), Jeremy M. Lange; 98–99 (UP), cynoclub/Adobe Stock; 98–99 (LO), Paul Cotney/Shutterstock; 98 (icon), artyway/Adobe Stock; 100–101, eurobanks/Shutterstock; 102 (UP LE), Ermolaev Alexander/Shutterstock; 102 (UP CTR), bestv/Shutterstock; 102 (LO RT), lalalululala/Adobe Stock; 102 (LO CTR), amKanobi/Shutterstock; 102 (LO LE), chaoss/Adobe Stock; 103 (UP), Eric Isselée/Adobe Stock; 103 (LO RT), Leigh Prather/Adobe Stock; 103 (LO LE), Mike Flippo/Shutterstock; 104 (LE), wayne/Adobe Stock; 104 (LO RT), Pim Leijen/Shutterstock; 105 (UP), russell102/Adobe Stock; 105 (LO RT), WildMedia/Adobe Stock; 105 (LO LE), Helen E. Grose/Shutterstock; 106–107, NG Maps; 106 (UP), evgenii/Adobe Stock; 106 (LE), lazyllama/Adobe Stock; 106 (LO), Manoj Shah/Getty Images; 107 (UP LE), Okssi/Adobe Stock; 107 (UP RT), Alexandra/Adobe Stock; 107 (LO RT), Grispb/Adobe Stock; 107 (LO LE), NIraelanor/Shutterstock; 108 (UP), Michael Kraus/Shutterstock; 108 (LO RT), Willee Cole/Adobe Stock; 108 (gold), Ron Dale/Shutterstock; 108 (LO LE), Chalabala/Adobe Stock; 109 (UP), Patryk Kosmider/Adobe Stock; 109 (LO RT), tanuha2001/Shutterstock; 109 (LO LE), Willee Cole/Adobe Stock; 110 (UP), adamkaz/Getty Images; 110 (LO RT), Evrymmnt/Adobe Stock; 110 (LO LE), cynoclub/Adobe Stock; 111 (UP), bobbymn/Getty Images; 111 (CTR), Itsanan/Adobe Stock; 111 (LO), Colin & Linda McKie/Adobe Stock; 112–113, Ivanova N/Shutterstock; 113 (UP), nelik/Shutterstock; 114 (UP), Christian Müller/Adobe Stock; 114 (LO RT), hramovnick/Adobe Stock; 114 (LO LE), Happy monkey/Adobe Stock; 115 (UP LE), Damedeeso/Dreamstime; 115 (UP RT), cynoclub/Adobe Stock; 115 (LO RT), Eric Isselée/Shutterstock; 115 (LO LE), Images by Dr. Alan Lipkin/Shutterstock; 116, Gennadiy Poznyakov/Adobe Stock; 117 (UP), Lisa Manuzak Wiley; 117 (paper), spacezerocom/Shutterstock; 117 (prints), FourLeafLover/Adobe Stock; 118–119, augustcindy/Adobe Stock; 120 (UP RT), thekopmylife/Getty Images; 120 (UP LE), BW Folsom/Shutterstock; 120 (LO), Cheryl E. Davis/Shutterstock; 121 (UP), Mary Swift/Adobe Stock; 121 (taco), Miguel Garcia Saavedra/Shutterstock; 121 (LO), fongleon356/iStockPhoto/Getty Images; 122–123, GVictoria/Adobe Stock; 125, Jakub Krechowicz/Adobe Stock; 128, adogslifephoto/Adobe Stock

ACKNOWLEDGMENTS

TO LINDA AND MARTHA, LOYAL FRIENDS AND FELLOW DOG LOVERS. —M.R.D.

TO CHI CHI, MY CHIHUAHUA, FOR ALL HE HAS TAUGHT ME. —S.G.

Since 1888, the National Geographic Society has funded more than 14,000 research, conservation, education, and storytelling projects around the world. National Geographic Partners distributes a portion of the funds it receives from your purchase to National Geographic Society to support programs including the conservation of animals and their habitats. To learn more, visit natgeo.com/info.

For more information, visit nationalgeographic.com, call 1-877-873-6846, or write to the following address:

National Geographic Partners, LLC
1145 17th Street NW
Washington, DC 20036-4688 U.S.A.

For librarians and teachers: nationalgeographic.com/books/librarians-and-educators

More for kids from National Geographic: natgeokids.com

National Geographic Kids magazine inspires children to explore their world with fun yet educational articles on animals, science, nature, and more. Using fresh storytelling and amazing photography, *Nat Geo Kids* shows kids ages 6 to 14 the fascinating truth about the world—and why they should care. **natgeo.com/subscribe**

For rights or permissions inquiries, please contact National Geographic Books Subsidiary Rights: bookrights@natgeo.com

Library of Congress Cataloging-in-Publication Data

Names: Donohue, Moira Rose, author. / Gibeault, Stephanie, author.
Title: Can't get enough dog stuff / Moira Rose Donohue, Stephanie Gibeault.
Description: Washington, D.C. : National Geographic Kids, [2023] | Series: Can't get enough | Includes index. | Audience: Ages 7-10 | Audience: Grades 2-3
Identifiers: LCCN 2022003535 | ISBN 9781426373770 (paperback) | ISBN 9781426374357 (library binding)
Subjects: LCSH: Dogs--Juvenile literature.
Classification: LCC SF426.5 .D66 2023 | DDC 636.7--dc23/eng/20220203
LC record available at https://lccn.loc.gov/2022003535

Acknowledgments
The publisher wishes to thank the book team: Paige Towler, editor; Michelle Harris, fact-checker; Shelby Lees, senior editor; Emily Fego, editorial assistant; Sarah J. Mock, senior photo editor; Eva Absher-Schantz, Director Art & Design; and Gus Tello, designer.

Printed in Hong Kong
22/PPHK/1